FUN FACTS THAT HAPPEN EVERY 60 SECONDS

STEVE MURRIE
AND
MATTHEW MURRIE

ILLUSTRATED BY
MARY ANNE LLOYD

SCHOLASTIC REFERENCE

An imprint of

SCHOLASTIC

Acknowledgments

The authors would like to thank the people at Scholastic for believing so strongly in and their enthusiasm for *Every Minute on Earth*. They would also like to give special thanks to the following, without whom the book would have been impossible: God's grace; Nancy for her proofreading and guidance; Dan, Holli, Libby, Andrew, and Seungah for their constant support; and their editor, Brenda Murray, for all of her help and patience.

Text copyright © 2007 by Steve and Matthew Murrie
Illustration copyright © 2007 by Scholastic Inc.
All rights reserved. Published by Scholastic Inc.
SCHOLASTIC, SCHOLASTIC REFERENCE, and associated logos are trademarks and/or registered trademarks of Scholastic Inc.

ISBN-13: 978-0-439-90887-0
ISBN-10: 0-439-90887-6

10 9 8 7 6 5 4 3 2   07 08 09 10 11

Printed in the U.S.A.
First printing, September 2007
Illustrated by Mary Anne Lloyd
Book design by Edward Miller

Contents

Introduction

How many times have you been asked the question: "What's happening?" And you shrugged your shoulders and answered, "Not much." You've probably had this conversation more than once today, not to mention the first ten minutes you are at school, the first phone call you receive on the weekend, and every time you meet someone new. The truth is that thousands of things are happening every minute of every day on Earth. You might be surprised to discover how much really happens: the number of lightning strikes, the amount of water going over Niagara Falls, how far the Earth travels, how much a whale can inhale, how many miles the fastest plane can travel, all in just one minute.

What is the origin of the minute? The Babylonians divided the period from sunrise to sunset into twelve equal parts called hours. By the 1700s clock makers were able to divide the hours into smaller units. They called their units *minutes*, which comes from the Roman word *minuta*, meaning small part. A minute may be a small unit of time, but it contains an enormous amount of happenings.

Minute can also mean very small or extremely small in size, or so small as to be insignificant. In this case it is pronounced "my noot" instead of "minnit." For instance, a grain of salt or the period at the end of a sentence is "my noot," whereas the amount of time it has taken you to read this paragraph is a "minnit."

Some of the "minnit" facts listed in this book are estimations because things can change from day to day and year to year. The facts that will probably change the most over time are the ones in the Technology, Pop Culture, Food, and Sports chapters. For the most part, the facts about the Human Body, Earth, and Space will probably remain the same indefinitely.

It has been said, "It is not the minutes we remember but the moments." Moments are special times when very significant things happen in our lives, such as when you hear that you have a new baby sister or brother. It could also be when you win an event or are recognized for some special achievement.

Time marches on. We cannot stop it or even slow it down, but we can stop and slow down to spend time with our family and friends, explore nature, and read to expand our world.

Make every minute count.

Where did we find all of this information?

That is a great question. Most of the information we found was on websites, encyclopedias, magazines, textbooks, and other fact books. We felt that it was important to present the facts in a new and innovative approach. The next time you are online, reading a book, or watching a TV program, chances are that someone is going to mention that in a minute so many things are made, something can go so far, or an animal can do so much.

EARTH

Did you feel that? **You probably didn't, but five earthquakes occur every minute.** Every day, there are 1,100 earthquakes that are strong enough to be felt. Eighty percent of the earthquakes occur under and around the Pacific Ocean, where the tectonic plates are spreading, colliding, and sliding under or by one another. Japan experiences around 1,500 earthquakes that are strong enough to be felt. Southern California has more than 10,000 earthquakes a year; only 15 to 20 are a magnitude 4, which can be felt by people both indoors and outdoors. The instrument that measures earthquake strength is called a seismometer. The most sensitive seismometers can measure a .0000039 inch (0.0000001 meter) movement of the earth. Earthquake strength is measured on the Richter scale, with 1 being the weakest and 10 the strongest.

Sound travels through air 67,500 feet (20,574 meters) or 12.8 miles (20.6 kilometers) a minute.

Jet planes can travel several times the speed of sound. The speed record for a plane is held by the now retired SR-71 Blackbird, which went 2,070 miles (3,330.6 kilometers) per hour. That is Mach 2.7, which is 2.7 times the speed of sound. The loudest sound heard by a human in recorded history was the eruption of the volcano Krakatau (Indonesia) in 1883. The eruption was heard 2,908 miles (4,679 kilometers) away by people on Rodrigues Island in the middle of the Indian Ocean. The loudest sound made by animals is the 188-decibel "song" of the fin whale and the blue whale. Scientists have detected these songs from more than 530 miles (852.8 kilometers) away.

Wow! Did you see that shooting star? Shooting stars are really not stars at all, but meteoroids that enter Earth's atmosphere. **Thousands of meteoroids are striking the atmosphere every minute of the day and night.** When we see them glowing in the sky, meteoroids are called meteors. We see them at night because they heat up until they glow as they pass through the atmosphere. If they are large enough, you can even see them during daylight as they get hot enough to glow as they pass through the atmosphere. When they land on Earth, they are called meteorites. The Hoba West Meteorite is the largest meteorite ever discovered and is 9 feet (2.7 meters) by 8 feet (2.4 meters) and weighs an estimated 130,000 pounds (59,090 kilograms) or 65 tons (9.1 metric tons). The meteorite was discovered at Hoba West, Namibia, in Africa in 1920 and has not been moved since it landed 80,000 years ago.

In one minute, 45,000,000 gallons (170,343,000 liters) of water go over Niagara Falls in North America.

Niagra Falls is made up of three separate falls: the American, Bridal Veil, and Canadian (Horseshoe) Falls. The American Falls is eroding away less than an inch (2.5 centimeters) a year and the Horseshoe Falls is eroding less than a foot (30.5 centimeters) a year. Before 1905, the Horseshoe Falls receded 3.8 feet (1.2 meters) a year. Between 1905 and 1925, the Horseshoe Falls eroded 2.3 feet (0.7 meter). Since then, some of the water has been diverted to a power plant to make electricity. During the nighttime hours from November 1 to March 31, more than 42,000,000 gallons (158,760,000 liters) are diverted to the power station, and only about 18,000,000 gallons (68,040,000 liters) go over the falls. Less water going over the Niagara Falls means less erosion of the falls' bedrock.

Talk about a big mouth! The mouth of the Amazon River is 90 miles (144.8 kilometers) wide and 300 feet (91.4 meters) deep where it empties into the Atlantic Ocean. During the wet season an average of 3.3 billion gallons (12.5 billion liters) of water empty into the ocean from the Amazon River every minute. The Amazon carries more water than the Mississippi, Nile, and Yangtze rivers combined. Amazingly, the Amazon River falls more than 16,400 feet (4,998.7 meters) in its first 600 miles (965.4 kilometers) from its source in the Andes Mountains. Then, it drops only 800 feet (243.8 meters) for the remaining 3,400 miles (5,470.6 kilometers) of its journey. When the Amazon empties its water into the Atlantic Ocean, the ocean water does not become salty for several miles. However, the Atlantic Ocean does turn brown from all the sediment in the river water it is carrying.

☼ EVERY MINUTE ON EARTH ☼

Have you ever heard someone say, "He is blowing off a little steam"? Well, that's what geysers do. Old Faithful is the best-known geyser in Yellowstone National Park, but it is only one of 200 active geysers in the park. **Every 65 minutes, crowds gather to watch Old Faithful erupt for four minutes.** In reality, Yellowstone's Excelsior Geyser is probably the most faithful, because it spews out thousands of gallons (liters) of near boiling water. Excelsior Geyser bubbles forth about 4,500 gallons (17,010 liters) of water at 199°F (93°C) every minute, which is 6 million gallons (11.3 million liters) a day. When it was active, Excelsior Geyser was the largest active geyser in the world, with an eruption 300 feet (91.4 meters) high and 300 feet (91.4 meters) wide. It is believed that years of erupting damaged the internal plumbing of the geyser and now it no longer spews water into the air, but is just a hot spring that is continuously bubbling.

Which is moving faster, Earth as it travels around the sun or a high-power rifle bullet? Amazingly Earth is moving more than 20 times faster in its orbit than the rifle bullet. **Earth revolves around, or orbits, the sun at the speed of 1,111 miles (1,787.6 kilometers) a minute.** Earth is also moving in other ways. It is always rotating (turning) on its axis, like a ball spinning on the ground. It rotates on its axis 18 miles (30 kilometers) every minute. However, different parts of Earth's surface travel at different speeds. The points on the equator travel fastest. As latitudes increase, getting closer to the North and South Poles, the speed of rotation decreases, until there is virtually no movement at either pole.

Can you imagine 51 football fields mowed in one minute? When you look at a football field you see one acre (0.4 hectare). **The tropical forests are being cut down at the rate of 51 acres (20.6 hectares) every minute of every day.** Unlike football fields that are mostly grass, tropical rain forests consist of huge trees and abundant wildlife species. They are being cleared for farming crops, raising livestock, and cutting timber at an alarming rate. Even though the tropical rain forests have a great deal of vegetation, the soil is very poor. The reason plants grow so well there is the amount of rainfall and the rapid rate of decomposition of the leaf litter. The Amazon tropical rain forest is the best known, but it is not the only one. There are other tropical rain forests in Central America, Africa, and Asia. The United States has tropical rain forests in Hawaii and even a temperate rain forest along the coast of Oregon, Washington State, and Alaska.

In the world, 55,555 barrels (2.3 million gallons or 8.7 million liters) of crude oil are being consumed every minute.

Although the world's demand for oil is increasing every day, the supply is limited and not renewable. By the year 2015, it is estimated that the world will be using 68,056 barrels, which is 400,000 gallons (1,514,165 liters) every minute. You might be wondering, how much oil is 1 million gallons (3.8 million liters)? It takes two city water towers to hold that quantity of water. So imagine two city water towers being drained in one minute. Since crude oil is a nonrenewable resource, the world will eventually run out, possibly in your lifetime. Petroleum is another word for crude oil and is made from the Latin words *petra* (rock) and *oleum* (oil).

Carbon dioxide is a waste product your body produces when it uses the energy it gets from food. When fossil fuels like coal, oil, and natural gas are burned so we can use their energy, they, too, give off carbon dioxide as a waste product. **Every minute, 12,400 tons (11,272.7 metric tons) of carbon dioxide are added to the atmosphere by the burning of fossil fuels.** The problem is that carbon dioxide is a greenhouse gas that helps trap the heat from the sun and keeps it from escaping back into space. Some scientists are concerned that this trapped heat will warm up Earth. This warming of Earth is called the greenhouse effect. The good news is that green plants reduce the amount of carbon dioxide in the air by using it to make food and produce oxygen.

When you look at ocean water, you do not see all the microscopic plankton that live in the water. However, 450,875 tons (409,886 metric tons) of plankton are produced in the oceans every minute. Why is that important? Well, plankton, the green plants in the ocean, are the first step in the food chain of almost all ocean organisms. Without plankton, marine animals could not survive. The largest known animal, the blue whale, depends on one of the smallest animals, krill, for its food. The krill (a shrimplike animal) feeds on plankton. Phytoplankton, or green algae, use the sun's light energy to power the process of photosynthesis, which is the food-making and oxygen-making process in green plants. Surprisingly, it is plankton in the ocean and not the trees in the rain forest that supply Earth with most of its oxygen supply!

Gone fishing! That's how 15 to 20 million people begin their day in the fishing industry around the world. **They catch 171 tons (155.1 metric tons) of oceanic fish every minute of every day.** However, the ocean fisheries are in trouble. Nine of the 17 major ocean fisheries in the world are declining due to overfishing and pollution. This has given rise to a new kind of farming called "aquaculture," in which fish are raised on land in ponds and water-retention areas. Today, aquaculturists raise 220 species of fish and other seafood, which include shrimp, salmon, trout, catfish, scallops, giant clams, carp, and tilapia. With 16 million tons (14.5 metric tons) produced throughout the world, aquaculture more than outpaces wild catches from freshwater sources. It is believed that by 2010 aquaculture will provide 40 percent of the world's fish harvest.

The deserts are advancing 1.7 acres (0.7 hectare) or about 1.7 football fields every minute all over the world.

In five years, the Gobi Desert in China claimed 20,240 square miles (51,895.4 square kilometers), an area the size of the state of Pennsylvania. This growing desert is only 150 miles (241.4 kilometers) from Beijing. The Gobi is not the only desert advancing over semiarid lands. Nigeria, Africa's most populous country, is losing 867,000 acres (350,268 hectares) of rangeland and cropland to deserts each year. Scientists are not sure why the deserts are advancing all over the world. One theory is global warming. When this happens, the land receives less rainfall and higher temperatures. The dry land eventually turns into a desert.

Every minute, 6.2 pounds (2.8 kilograms) of soil dust enters the atmosphere.

Have you ever been in a dust storm? Not the one that happens when the wind stirs up a little dust on a playground, but one that completely covers the sky. During the Dust Bowl of the 1930s, 3 to 4 inches (7.6 to 10.2 centimeters) of topsoil disappeared in many places because of the wind. Overgrazing by livestock and overcultivation are the main causes for soil lost to wind erosion. When plant cover is removed from the soil, there is nothing to hold the soil in place. So when the wind comes through, it picks up the loose soil particles and they enter the atmosphere.

When you flushed the toilet today, you added 1.6 to 7 gallons to the 6.8 billion gallons (25.7 billion liters) of water flushed every day in the United States. **The estimated total water use of the United States is 480 billion gallons (1.8 trillion liters) every minute.** The breakdown of water usage in the United States is 69 percent for agriculture, 28 percent for industry, and only 8 percent for drinking, bathing, and watering lawns and plants. Water plays an important role in producing our food. It takes 6 gallons (22.7 liters) to make a single serving of lettuce, and a single tomato needs 8 gallons (30.2 liters). Even an 8-ounce (31.5-milliliter) glass of milk takes 49 gallons (185.2 liters) of water to produce, which includes water for the cow, water for the grass to grow, and water needed to process the milk.

Planet Earth receives 907 million tons (824.5 million metric tons) of rainfall every minute.

Earth is a very large place and, in some places on Earth, it is raining right this very minute. If you really like rain, you could move to Mount Waialeale in Hawaii. It rains 350 days out of the 365 days in a year, for an average yearly rainfall of 33 feet (10.1 meters). If you detest rain, you could move to Quillagua, which is located in the Atacama Desert in Chile. For a period of 37 years, it only had 0.02 inches (0.5 millimeter) of rain. Some tropical regions have rainy seasons called monsoons, when it rains almost daily for six months. Then, during the next six months of the year, it is the dry season with very little rain.

It is hard to believe, but there are 2,000 thunderstorms occurring on Earth every minute. In those thousands of thunderstorms, lightning is striking Earth at an alarming rate of 6,000 times a minute. Lightning is a gigantic discharge of static electricity that is caused by air moving in a cloud. Thunder is produced when the lightning superheats the air to almost five times the temperature of the sun. This sudden heating causes the air to compress faster than the speed of sound and forms a shock wave that we hear as thunder. You can determine how far away a thunderstorm is by counting the seconds between the lightning flash and the thunder, then dividing by five. If you hear thunder ten seconds after the flash, the storm is 2 miles (3.2 kilometers) away.

A solar eclipse travels across Earth's equator at 18 miles (29 kilometers) a minute.

A solar eclipse occurs when the moon travels between the sun and Earth. The moon and the sun appear to be the same size in the sky, even though the moon is 400 times smaller than the sun. This is because the moon is 400 times closer to Earth than the sun is. When the sun is completely blocked out by the moon, it is called a total solar eclipse. Only a small part of Earth is covered by a total solar eclipse. On a larger part of Earth's surface, a partial solar eclipse is observed. The sun's light is usually blocked out completely for 2.5 minutes, but eclipses have lasted as long as 7 minutes and 40 seconds.

How would you like to go to a nice quiet restaurant for dinner and watch a volcano erupting? Well, you can if you travel to Costa Rica. That is where you will find Arenal, the second most active volcano in the world. Nearby, in the town of La Fortuna, there are restaurants that offer spectacular views of the volcano erupting. Other constantly erupting volcanoes are Kilauea in Hawaii, Stromboli in Italy, Ambrim in Vanuata, Merapi in Indonesia, Masaya in Nicaragua, and Unzen in Japan. **These seven volcanoes are erupting every minute of every day.** Most of the eruptions are not violent, earthshaking ones, but ones where either lava is flowing out quietly or steam and gases are fuming out the crater. Vulcanologists, scientists who study volcanoes, have even devised a Volcano Explosivity Index (VEI) that measures the relative strength of volcano eruptions on a scale from 1 to 10.

Can you even imagine an ocean wave that reaches the height of 1,719 feet (524 meters)? That's higher than the tallest building in the world, Taipei 101 (Taiwan), which is 1,470 feet (448.1 meters). It happened on July 9, 1958, in Lituya Bay, Alaska. What would have caused such a colossal wave? You guessed it. It was a tsunami. A tsunami can travel much faster and with much more power than an ocean wave. Tsunamis are created by extremely strong forces under the ocean. They can be caused by earthquakes, volcano eruptions, and landsides that occur underwater. The speed of an ocean wave is 0.9 mile (1.5 kilometers) per minute, but a tsunami travels 9.8 miles (15.8 kilometers) a minute.

The Lituya Bay tsunami was caused by an earthquake measuring 7.9 on the Richter scale that created a giant wave that sent water 3,600 feet (1,097.3 meters) inland and knocked down millions of trees.

Do you get excited about dirt? Most people don't, but scientists and farmers do because they know how important dirt, or soil, is to the well-being of every person on Earth. Around the world, soil is being carried away 10 to 40 times faster than it is being replaced. Soil erosion is destroying cropland equal to the size of Indiana every year. Controlling soil loss is very simple; the soil can be covered with cover crops when the land is not being used to grow food crops.

More than 2,103 tons (1,907.8 metric tons) of topsoil is being lost in the United States every minute due to water erosion. The Mississippi River alone dumps 500 million tons (454.5 metric tons) of soil into the Gulf of Mexico every year.

Are people the only entities that produce natural gas, or methane? No, bacteria and other life-forms are converting our trash into 95.4 tons (86.7 metric tons) of methane gas in landfills every minute. Organisms in rice paddies get into the action by producing 143 tons (130 metric tons) of methane a minute. Cattle are producing methane that comes out both ends at the rate of 190 tons (172.7 metric tons) each minute. Termites, one of the most abundant animals on Earth, are generating 38 tons (34.5 metric tons) every minute. Some landfills are being "mined" for the methane they produce, which is piped to factories and facilities that use the gas for fuel to heat their plants.

When it rains an inch (2.5 centimeters) in the city limits of Atlanta, Georgia, 1.6 million gallons (6 million liters) of water fall. That is a lot of water, but the greatest daily rainfall ever recorded was 73 inches (1.9 meters). It occurred at Cilaos, Reunion Island, in the Indian Ocean on March 15–16, 1952. That was 116 million gallons (438.5 million liters) of water. The greatest yearly rainfall was 4,678 inches (11.9 meters) at Mawsynram, Meghazaya, India. That is 390 feet (118.9 meters), which is taller than the tallest redwood tree. Rain is not the only form of precipitation—snow also falls from clouds. One inch (2.5 centimeters) of rain is equal to approximately 10 inches (25.4 centimeters) of snow.

The wind in an average jet stream is going 3.3 miles (5.3 kilometers) per minute and in the fastest jet stream the speed is 6.7 miles (10.8 kilometers) per minute. A jet stream is a narrow, fast-flowing air current in the upper atmosphere. The average speeds of jet streams are 250 miles (402.3 kilometers) per hour. The fastest ever measured was above South Uist, Outer Hebrides, United Kingdom, at an altitude of 154,200 feet (47,000.3 meters) on December 13, 1967. This jet stream was going 408 miles (656.5 kilometers) per hour. By comparison, commercial jet planes go about 500 miles (804.5 kilometers) per hour and the highest wind speed in a tornado is only 300 miles (482.7 kilometers) per hour.

How can a powder avalanche hurt someone? Isn't powder soft? Well, getting hit by anything traveling more than 220 miles (354 kilometers) per hour can cause some damage. **A powder avalanche can travel 4.2 miles (6.8 kilometers) in a minute.** A powder avalanche is the largest and most destructive kind of avalanche. It begins when a rock or ice block falls into a mass of loosely packed snow. The snow mass begins to fall while riding on a cushion of air at high speeds. A blast of air precedes the powder avalanche, knocking down things in its path. Then tons (metric tons) of powder batter whatever remains.

Interesting Facts:

- Vibration from a loud noise can trigger a powder avalanche.
- France suffers 21 percent of all avalanche deaths, followed by Austria, the United States, and Switzerland.

Do all planets spin on their axes at the same speed? Would you believe that there is a planet that spins more than 27 times faster than Earth? No, it is not Mercury, the smallest planet, or Pluto, a dwarf planet. It is Jupiter, the largest planet. Jupiter spins 28,325 miles (44,574.9 kilometers) per hour. Saturn is the second fastest with a speed of 22,892 miles (36,833.2 kilometers) per hour. Wow! The largest planets spin the fastest. **By comparison, Earth spins at 1,040 miles (1,673.6 kilometers) per hour, which breaks down to 16 miles (25.7 kilometers) a minute for a person standing on Earth's equator.** A person standing on Jupiter's equator would be going 472 miles (759.4 kilometers) a minute.

South Africa mines produce 22.3 pounds (10.1 kilograms) of gold every minute.

The United States follows in second with 13.5 pounds (6.1 kilograms) a minute. Have you ever wondered why gold is so valuable? To start with, it has an attractive, vivid yellow color. All the rest of the metals, except for copper, are silver-colored. Gold is also extremely rare. It is estimated that all the gold in the world would fit in a cube 72 feet (21.9 meters) long on each side. Four Olympic-size swimming pools could hold all the gold ever found. Gold is very soft. You can bite it and leave teeth marks. Gold is malleable, which means it can be hammered into extremely thin sheets. About 100,000 sheets of gold can be made from a 1-inch (2.5-centimeter) cube of gold.

Interesting Facts:

- The Egyptians mined gold as early as 2000 B.C.
- Gold is found on all continents except Antarctica, where mining is prohibited.

Can you tell the difference between grains of sand and newly mined diamonds? They look identical. The diamonds most people are familiar with are the ones that have been cut and polished. Diamonds look like sand grains when they come out of the ground. **Diamonds are found at the rate of 50 grams (250 carats) a minute.** The approximate worth of 50 grams of diamonds is $17,170. Russia is the largest producer of diamonds with 38.4 million carats in 2006.

Interesting Facts:

- Two million people work in the diamond industry from mining to the making of 67 million pieces of jewelry each year.
- Diamonds are probably the oldest things you will ever own; they are estimated to have been formed 3 billion years ago.

☀ EARTH ☀

Activity 1

Make Your Own One-Minute Timer

Did you know that you can make your own one-minute timer? All you need is a sheet of paper, tape, table salt, a plastic water or soda bottle, and a clock with a second hand. First, make a funnel out of the paper by folding it in half from top to bottom. Next, curl the ends around each other, making a 1/4-inch (0.5 cm) hole at the bottom and a 3-inch (8 cm) opening at the top. Tape the edges together. Hold your finger over the hole and pour about 1/2 cup (125 ml) of table salt in the top opening. Place the funnel over the plastic bottle and look at the clock. When the second hand gets to the 12, remove your finger and let the salt fall into the bottle. When one minute is up, put your finger back on the hole and throw away the excess salt. Next, pour the salt in the bottle back into the funnel. Now you have your own one-minute timer.

Activity 2

Country Memory Challenge

Grab a globe or get online and study the countries on one of the continents for one minute. Then see how many you can name without looking in one minute. Not enough of a challenge? Next time, try writing the countries out; only count the countries you spell correctly. Once you've mastered the countries on the 6 continents (sorry, Antarctica, no country can claim you), repeat this activity with capital cities instead of countries. How many can you get? Once you become a pro, challenge members of your family or your friends.

Comets near the sun travel 1,440 miles (2,317 kilometers) per minute, but comets near the dwarf planet Pluto travel at 72 miles (115.8 kilometers) per minute. As comets get near the sun, the gravitational attraction of the sun increases dramatically. They travel faster and faster. If a comet picks up enough speed, it will either completely melt or it will crash into the sun. Astronomers who study the sun actually have pictures of comets striking the sun. Recently, a comet crashed into the planet Jupiter and astronomers captured the event on video. As some comets travel to the outer edge of our solar system near the orbit of Pluto, they slow down.

The solar system moves around the Milky Way galaxy at a speed of 9,000 miles (14,481 kilometers) a minute.

The Milky Way galaxy is speeding through the cosmos at 22,200 miles (35,719.8 kilometers) per minute. Our solar system is located in one of the outer spiral arms of the Milky Way galaxy. The arms of the galaxy are turning like the blades on a pinwheel. Even though when we see the Milky Way galaxy, it appears stationary in the night sky, it is really turning around a central axis.

The sun is located about 26,000 light-years from the galactic center. A light-year is roughly 5.9 trillion miles (9.5 trillion kilometers). The sun's orbit around the Milky Way is about 150,000 light-years in distance. The sun takes about 225 million years to revolve around the galactic center.

DID YOU FEEL THAT?

A space shuttle has to travel 416 miles (669.3 kilometers) per minute to escape the powerful tug of Earth's gravity.

It takes the shuttle only eight minutes to accelerate to that speed. A space shuttle is officially a space transportation system (STS). The *Orbiter* is the name of the airplane-like craft in which the astronauts are stationed. When the STS is launched, it is going straight up for a few hundred feet (meters) before it turns and takes a slanted course. By doing this, its forward speed can increase to the 416 miles (669.3 kilometers) a minute needed to escape Earth's gravity faster than if it were going straight up.

The *International Space Station (ISS)* is traveling 289 miles (465 kilometers) every minute in its orbit around Earth. When the people on the *ISS* look down on Earth, the planet appears to be moving slowly beneath them. The *ISS* is moving extremely fast, however. It is similar to watching the ground when flying in an airplane. The ground appears to move very slowly even though the plane is probably moving more than 500 miles (804.5 kilometers) per hour. The *ISS* is covering the same 500 miles (804.5 kilometers) in less than two minutes.

Interesting Facts:

- The *ISS*'s living space is larger than a five-room house.
- The *ISS* weighs 1 million pounds (454,545.5 kilos).
- The main section of the *ISS* is 361 feet (110 meters), which is longer than a football field including the end zones.
- The 55-foot (16.8-meter) robot arm of the *ISS* can lift the 110-ton (100-metric ton) space shuttle.

Every minute, the planet Mercury, which is the closest to the sun, goes 1,782 miles (2,873 kilometers) per hour in its orbit around the sun.

The dwarf planet Pluto, which is the farthest from the sun, goes 177 miles (285 kilometers) per hour in its orbit around the sun. The planets closer to the sun have to have more speed or they will be pulled into the sun by its tremendous gravitational force. Even though Mercury is speedy, it is not the fastest natural body in space. The comets and asteroids that orbit the sun are faster, and those that get the closest to the sun without crashing into it are the fastest in the solar system.

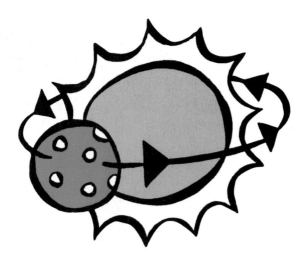

How would you feel if you gained 167.9 tons (152.6 metric tons) every minute of the day and night?

That is exactly what happens to Earth. Every time you go outside, small pieces of comets, space dust, and micrometeorites might be falling on your head. Space dust of all kinds and sizes fills the space that Earth travels through every year. Lucky for us, most of it burns up as meteors as it enters Earth's atmosphere at extremely high speeds. Most space dust is less than 0.04 inches (1 millimeter) in diameter and can be composed of rock, metal, or both. You can take part in a project to collect sky dust at www.skydust.org using a strong magnet, a magnifying glass or microscope, and runoff from your home's roof.

45

☼ **SPACE** ☼

Does space have a graveyard? Yes, it does but not all dead satellites are "buried" there. **Most of the 8,000 dead, broken, and damaged satellites are circling Earth every minute.** Satellites in geostationary orbit revolve above the equator in the same direction and with the exact speed of Earth. Many satellites are kept in this position because fixed antennae on Earth can keep in touch with them easily. However, unlike dead satellites in a low Earth orbit, which will finally fall back to Earth as a result of atmospheric drag, and burn up, geostationary satellites experience no drag and do not fall back to Earth. To keep dead geostationary satellites from interfering with working satellites in geostationary orbit, they are boosted 180 miles (289.6 kilometers) to a higher orbit, which is called the graveyard.

You had better be prepared to wait a long time if you say, "Wait a minute" when you are on the dwarf planet Pluto. **A minute on Pluto is equal to 248.5 Earth minutes because its year is 248.5 Earth years long.** However, that may be the least of your worries because at current spacecraft travel speeds it will take you about nine years to get to Pluto. Once you get there you had better have a warm spacesuit, because the temperature will be almost a constant minus 400°F (minus 240°C). In addition to water and oxygen, leaded boots might be needed. The gravity is one-fifteenth of Earth's gravity so a 100-pound (45.5-kilogram) person would only weigh a little less than 7 pounds (3.2 kilograms)!

What would you think if you saw hundreds of shooting stars streaking through the sky every minute? Well, that happened in North America on November 18, 1966, at four o'clock in the morning. It was the most spectacular meteor shower in recent times. Actually, it was called a meteor storm because there was more than 1 meteor a second, or 1,000 per hour. Every year in mid-November, Earth travels through a stream of gas, dust, and rocks left behind by Comet Tempel-Tuttle. This comet passes Earth's orbit around every 33 years, leaving more debris with each pass. The resulting meteor shower is called the Leonid meteor shower because the meteors seem to shoot out of the constellation Leo. **A Leonid meteorite can enter Earth's atmosphere at 2,647 miles (4,259 kilometers) a minute, which is 133 times the top speed of an F-18 jet fighter.**

The last time Comet Tempel-Tuttle passed through Earth's orbit was January 1998.

932 MPH

The average speed of an asteroid is 932 miles (1,500 kilometers) a minute. Most asteroids are in an orbit between the planets Mars and Jupiter called the "Asteroid Belt." Several thousand asteroids have been discovered and thousands more are discovered every year. There are 26 known asteroids with diameters of 120 miles (193.1 kilometers) and probably 1 million asteroids in the 0.6-mile (1-kilometer) range. Not all asteroids are in the Asteroid Belt; some asteroids have orbits that cross Earth's orbit. These are called "Near Earth Asteroids" (NEAs). The 800 asteroids that get very close to Earth are called "Potentially Hazardous Asteroids" (PHAs).

The outer winds of Jupiter's Giant Red Spot are spinning at 5.8 miles (9.3 kilometers) a minute.

The best-known feature of the planet Jupiter is the Giant Red Spot near its equator. It is believed to be some kind of hurricane because hurricanes on Earth have a similar pattern. However, the Giant Red Spot has lasted for more than 300 years. British observer Robert Hooke discovered it in 1664 using a telescope. Newsflash! A new red spot has been discovered by a Philippine amateur astronomer, Christopher Go. Mr. Go observed that the color of a newly formed white oval had turned brick red on February 27, 2006. He had watched the birth of a new red spot, which is called "Red Spot Junior."

Interesting Facts:

- The Giant Red Spot is moving east and Red Spot Junior is moving west.
- Lightning is present in the Giant Red Spot.
- Two to three Earths could fit inside the Giant Red Spot.

The sun converts 240 million tons (218.2 million metric tons) of matter into energy every minute.

Is the sun burning up? Not exactly. It is undergoing thermonuclear fusion, in which the sun's hydrogen gas is being converted into helium gas and energy. It takes a million degrees of temperature to start this process and a tremendous amount of heat energy is released. This contributes more heat, which adds up to higher temperatures, and thus the process continues. The sun is extremely massive. More than a thousand Earths could go across its diameter, and it would take more than a million Earths to fill the volume of the sun. It is estimated that the sun has enough hydrogen to keep "burning" for more than 3 billion years.

Did you watch cable TV today? Cable TV companies use communication satellites to transmit their programs. **These communication satellites are traveling 54 miles (86.9 kilometers) a minute at a height of 22,000 miles (35,405.6 kilometers) above Earth.** Approximately 20 communication satellites are launched each year. The average life of a communication satellite is about 20 years, which is up from 7 years in the 1980s. One danger to communication satellites is space debris. One of the U.S. Air Force Space Command Space Safety Office's missions is to keep communication satellites away from the more than 9,000 pieces of space debris and dead satellites. If they fail, millions of dollars of communication satellites would become worthless junk.

Every minute, 2,271 working satellites are orbiting Earth.

On a clear night, you might see a bright object very high in the sky move from west to east. It might be one of the 2,271 artificial (man-made) satellites orbiting Earth. Some of them are large enough and close enough to catch the sunlight and reflect it to Earth. These are the ones we see move across the sky. The communication satellites used for satellite TV are too far above Earth to see. They are approximately 20,000 miles (32,180 kilometers) high. At this height, their orbit speed is equal to the rotation of Earth, so they will remain stationary over the spot on Earth that sends TV signals to them.

The existence of galaxies was not known until 1924, when American astronomer Edwin Hubble discovered the galaxy Andromeda with his 100-inch (2.5-meter) telescope. Years later, the Hubble Space Telescope was created and named after Edwin Hubble. The Hubble Space Telescope has discovered many galaxies since it was put in orbit by the Discovery Space Shuttle on April 25, 1990. The Hubble Space Telescope has found that galaxies do collide, and in fact this is more the rule than the exception. **Around 1,800 galaxies are colliding with other galaxies every minute.** Galaxies contain millions and billions of individual stars. Remarkably, galaxies are so vast, and there is so much space between the individual stars, that it is quite possible that when two of them collide, none of the billions of stars in either galaxy hit one another.

Comet Hale-Bopp traveled 1,633 miles (2,627.5 kilometers) per minute at its closest orbit to the sun, but only traveled 4 miles (6.4 kilometers) a minute at its farthest point from the sun. Comet Hale-Bopp was discovered on July 23, 1995, by two astronomers in two different locations on the same night. Amateur astronomers Alan Hale in New Mexico and Thomas Bopp in Arizona discovered the comet near the orbit of Jupiter. Comet Hale-Bopp was 1,000 times brighter than the famous Comet Halley at that distance. The size of Comet Hale-Bopp is believed to be 25 to 44 miles (40.2 to 70.8 km) in diameter.

Interesting Facts:

- Comet Hale-Bopp came within 122 million miles (196.3 million kilometers) of Earth.
- Its tail was 50 to 60 million miles (80.5 to 96.5 million kilometers) long.

Did you know that there is a spacecraft carrying a gold record?
It is *Voyager 1* and it is currently traveling at 642 miles (1,033 kilometers) a minute out of the solar system and into deep space. *Voyager 1* was launched September 5, 1977, from Cape Canaveral, Florida. Its mission is to explore all of the outer planets—Jupiter, Saturn, Uranus, Neptune, and Pluto (now considered a dwarf planet)—as well as their 48 moons. The gold record on board is a greeting to any form of life *Voyager 1* might encounter. The 12-inch (30.5-centimeter) gold-plated copper disk contains sounds and images of life and culture on Earth. There are 115 images and natural sounds. It also includes spoken greetings from Earth people in 55 different languages.

What is one of the fastest-moving man-made objects?

The spacecraft *Helios 2* orbited the sun at 2,500 miles (4,022.5 kilometers) per minute or 150,000 miles (241,350 kilometers) per hour, which is the fastest any man-made object has traveled.

It reached its top speed on its closest approach to the sun, which was 28 million miles (45.1 million kilometers), due to the pull of the sun's gravity. *Helios 2* was launched in January 1976 as a joint venture between the United States and West Germany to study the sun.

Activity 1

Spinning Coins

The Earth is constantly moving; not just around the sun, but around its own axis as well. It is why we have night and day. The force of gravity is responsible for keeping your feet on the ground. In order to get an idea of how gravity works, grab a coin and set it on its edge then remove your finger. What happens? It probably fell. Now set it on its edge and give it a flick. As long as it is spinning, it remains upright. See how long you can get your coin to spin. Experiment with different surfaces and different coins—do dimes spin longer than quarters? Once you get good at spinning your coins, see how many you can get spinning at the same time. Can you get eight like the planets? Use larger coins for the giant planets and smaller ones for the little planets. Now you've got your own solar system.

Activity 2

Bubble Float

Soap bubbles are shaped like the eight planets: round and full of air. All of the planets are round, and the gas giants—Jupiter, Saturn, Uranus, and Neptune—are made mostly of air. Everyone who has ever blown a bubble knows that no bubble lasts forever. Typically, as soon as they come in contact with another object (usually the ground), they pop. However, if you have played with bubbles enough, you probably also know that waving the air around them can have an effect on their flight. But watch out: waving too strongly can also cause a gust of air forceful enough to burst the bubble. Your challenge is to blow a bubble and try to keep it in the air for at least a minute. You will need to keep it from falling while guiding it out of danger from nearby objects— all at the same time.

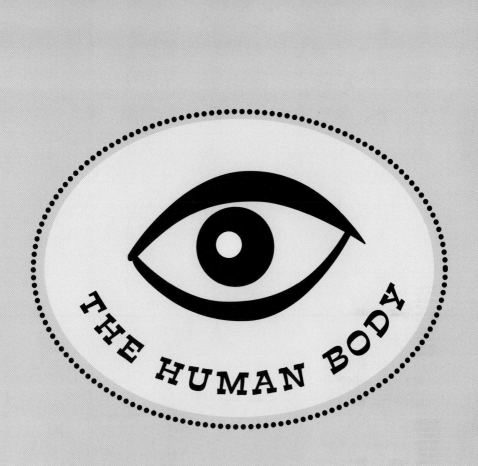

THE HUMAN BODY

The two kidneys in an adult's body produce 0.1 ounce (1 milliliter) of urine every minute, and they filter on average 1 ounce (10.4 milliliters) of blood each minute. When it is completely filled, the adult bladder can hold approximately 17 to 18 ounces (502.8 to 532.3 milliliters) of urine. A child's bladder can only hold 1 to 1.5 ounces, or 6 to 9 teaspoons (29.6 to 44.4 milliliters), per year of age. This explains why young children need to use the restroom more frequently than adults. The human kidneys are constantly working, filtering the blood of wastes and excess salt and water. An adult's kidneys filter about 50 gallons (190 liters) of blood each day.

The heart is constantly beating and pumping blood through the body. The adult human heart pumps 3.5 quarts (3.3 liters) of blood every minute of a person's life. That is almost a gallon (3.8 liters) of blood a minute. During hard exercise, it pumps between two and three times more. For an organ about the size of a person's fist, it is remarkable that it can pump so much blood for so many years. The adult female heart only weighs 9 ounces (254 grams), and the adult male heart weighs a mere 10.5 ounces (298 grams). The average human has thousands of miles (kilometers) of blood vessels in their body and most of the blood travels through several miles (kilometers) during a day.

Day and night, at rest or exercising, you are always breathing. **A person breathes an average of 15 times a minute during their waking hours.** The more active a person is, the more he or she needs to breathe. The lungs are made of a spongy tissue and do not have any muscles of their own. The diaphragm and the rib muscles are muscles responsible for breathing. During the breathing process, the rib muscles lift the rib cage up and out. At the same time, the diaphragm contracts and moves toward the abdomen, which creates a vacuum. The lungs move down and out to fill the vacuum and they inflate with air. When the diaphragm and rib muscles relax, the ribs collapse and air rushes out of the lungs.

BREATHE

A red blood cell will travel 27 feet (8.2 meters) in one minute.

After a red blood cell leaves the left side of the heart, it will travel through arteries, capillaries, and veins and then back to the right side of the heart. The cell travels the fastest in the arteries because of the greater pressure. It slows down to almost a standstill as it passes through the microscopic capillaries, then speeds up once it gets into the larger veins. The red blood cell can take many paths since there are 60,000 miles (96,540 kilometers) of blood vessels in the body. That is a distance equal to twice around the world at the equator.

Between 120 to 180 million red blood cells are made every minute, while the same number are being taken out of circulation. This seems like a very large number, which it is, but there can be 500 million red blood cells in 0.2 teaspoon (1 cubic centimeter) of blood. A cubic centimeter is about 10 drops of blood. Since the red blood cells travel several miles (kilometers) a day, they wear out sooner than other cells that do not have to travel. As the red blood cells go through the blood vessels, they are bumping into other red blood cells, white blood cells, platelets, and the walls of blood vessels. During this travel, they get "banged up" quite a bit and it takes its toll on their life span. Due to this, the marrow of the bone is producing millions of red blood cells by the minute. Bone marrow is located in the innermost part of the bone and is protected by the entire bone so it can do its important job without being damaged easily.

Every minute, 60 million white blood cells are being made and 60 million white blood cells die. White blood cells number between 400,000 and 1,100,000 per teaspoon (4.9 cubic centimeters) of blood, which makes up less than 1 percent of the total blood volume. In spite of the fact that white blood cells are outnumbered 90 to 1 by red blood cells, they serve as an important part of the body's immune system. They act as a police force in defending the body against damage caused by bacteria, viruses, parasites, and even tumor cells. Like the red blood cells, most white blood cells are formed in the bone marrow.

Every minute, 500,000 damaged stomach-lining cells are being replaced.

BURP

The reason so many cells are replaced is that the stomach is an acid-filled pit. Some stomach cells produce hydrochloric acid, a very strong acid that kills microorganisms and breaks down cell walls and connective tissue. The stomach wall is made of three layers of smooth muscle. These muscles are constantly contracting at about 3 contractions a minute. This mixes and churns the stomach contents. Mucous membranes line the stomach and secrete a thick, gooey liquid that protects the stomach from its own secretions (like acid). The cells of the mucous membrane wear out quickly, and the entire stomach lining is replaced every three days.

Each minute, 30,000 to 40,000 pieces of dead skin are lost.

Even though the skin is not typically thought of as an organ, like the kidney or liver, scientifically it is. In fact, the skin is the largest and heaviest organ the body has. In the average adult, it covers 21.5 square feet (2 square meters) and weighs 11 pounds (5 kilograms). Most of the skin on the body is 0.04 to 0.08 inch (1 to 2 millimeters) thick with thicker places on the hands and feet.

The outermost layer of skin is the epidermis. It is waterproof and tough, consisting of about 20 to 30 rows of tightly connected, flat, dead cells. It takes about 14 days for the cells to move from the inner layer of the epidermis to the outer layer. The dead cells stay there for another 14 days or so before flaking off. Those dead cells are the 30,000 to 40,000 that are being lost each minute.

It happened in the blink of an eye! Exactly how fast *is* the blink of an eye? Well, a blink lasts 100 to 150 milliseconds. **The average person blinks about 15 times a minute.** Blinking serves several useful purposes. When we blink, the eyeball surface is moistened, allowing oxygen to be absorbed by the cornea, which does not have its own blood supply to deliver it. In turn, the lens of the eye gets oxygen through the cornea. The lens is made up of approximately 35 percent protein and 65 percent water. The eyelid acts like a windshield wiper on a car, cleaning the eyeball surface of small airborne particles that land on the eye.

Interesting Fact:

• A person spends nine days blinking in a year.

Americans are passing 6,250 cubic feet (177 cubic meters) of gas every minute.

That is equal to a room 20 feet (6.1 meters) long by 20 feet (6.1 meters) wide by 16 feet (4.9 meters) high, or four average bedrooms. Every minute, 1,717,033 people on Earth are passing gas. The scientific name for gas is *flatus*, or flatulence. A flatus is made of a combination of gases: nitrogen, carbon dioxide, oxygen, methane, and hydrogen. Sometimes the gas escapes out the mouth when a person burps. The chemical that makes passed gas stink is hydrogen sulfide. This gas contains sulfur, so the more foods you eat that have sulfur the more your passed gas will stink. Cabbage, beans, cheese, soda, and eggs are known to have a lot of sulfur compounds. Healthy people will pass gas about 16 times a day. Dogs, cats, and cows pass gas, too. Elephants pass gas more than any other animal.

What's on your mind? If you answer "nothing," that's not quite true. **Your brain is sending and receiving 6 trillion messages every minute in order to keep your body working right.** The human brain has 1 trillion nerve cells and 100 trillion nerve connections that can process 600 quadrillion instructions a minute. Are you thinking about the digestion process that is occurring in your body this very minute? Probably not, but your brain is sending and receiving messages to all parts of your digestive system, like keeping your stomach churning its contents. Your brain is very active and alert at all times. Even while you sleep, it is sending and receiving messages. Your heart gets to rest between beats, but your brain never gets a break.

72

An adult can produce two-thirds of a cup (156 milliliters) of sweat during every minute of heavy exercise. That's not too surprising considering that there is an average of 2.3 million sweat glands in the human body. Men have more sweat glands than women. Sweat glands are distributed throughout the body, but most are located on the soles of the feet, the palms of the hands, the forehead, and the armpits. Each foot has 250,000 sweat glands and usually produces one pint (473 milliliters) of sweat a day. The palms of the hands have about 3,000 sweat glands per square inch (2.5 square centimeters). A sweat gland is made of a coiled tube of cells where the sweat is made and a straight, narrow tube, or duct, that carries the sweat to the surface of the skin.

Brisk walking burns 5 calories per minute, stair climbing can burn 10 calories a minute, and jumping rope burns 12.5 calories a minute.

Our bodies use food energy in order to carry out the processes needed to stay alive. A moderately active adolescent girl needs about 1,900 calories a day, and a moderately active adolescent boy will need 2,200 calories daily. The measure of how much energy is in food is called the calorie. If you exercise, you will use more calories, and the longer and harder you exercise the more calories you will burn. You may hear people talking about watching the calories they eat because they do not want to gain weight. A person will have to burn 3,500 calories to lose 1 pound (454.5 grams) of weight.

74

A fingernail grows 0.0000027 inch (0.0000069 centimeters) a minute.

A toenail grows at the rate of 0.0000009 inch (0.0000023 centimeters) a minute. It has been calculated that the fingernail grows 0.000000039 inch (1 nanometer) a second, which is the width of an average molecule. The middle fingernail grows the fastest, followed by the ring, index, and pinky fingers. The thumbnails grow the slowest. Fingernails begin to grow before birth. In the tenth week of human development, the fetus develops fingernails. By the fourteenth week toenails appear. The fingernails reach to the end of the digits in the thirty-second week.

A hair grows 0.00027 inch (0.00069 centimeters) a minute.

Hair grows out of a hair follicle. Each human head carries around 100,000 hair follicles. Some people have as many as 150,000. Each follicle can grow 20 new hairs in a person's lifetime. Not all of the follicles are growing hair at the same time. The hair follicles undergo a cycle of active growth and rest. The length the hair will grow depends on a person's age and on what part of the body the hair grows. A young person's hair may grow 3 feet (91.4 centimeters) or more before it stops and enters a resting stage. An older person's hair may only grow to shoulder length before it stops growing. The hairs on an adult scalp do not grow all at the same time so you are growing new hairs and losing about 50 to 100 hairs a day.

The human eardrum vibrates at 20 times a minute when a 20-hertz sound is heard.

The eardrum will vibrate more with a higher-pitched sound, up to 20,000 times a minute. The human ear is made of the outer ear, the middle ear, and the inner ear. The outer ear flap that you see is called the pinna, or auricle. It helps capture sound waves. The middle ear is only the size of a pea and contains the paper-thin eardrum and the three smallest bones in the body, the hammer, anvil, and stirrup. The inner ear has an organ that looks like a snail's shell, called the cochlea, which takes vibrations from the outside and turns them into electrical impulses that the brain can understand.

WHAT

The human vocal cords vibrate at 6,000 times a minute during speech.

The term "vocal cords" is rather misleading because the sound-producing parts are not really cords. They are folds of expandable tissues that extend across a hollow chamber, the voice box. When speaking, the vocal folds can vibrate more than 100 times a second, which is too fast to see. The surface layer of each vocal cord is loose enough to vibrate in a wavelike fashion. The thinner the vocal cords the faster they vibrate, producing a higher pitch. Most women and young children have thinner vocal cords. Men usually have thicker vocal cords and produce low-pitched sounds. The voice box, which contains the vocal cords, is a hollow tube 1.2 to 1.6 inches (3 to 4 centimeters) wide, made of cartilage and located at the top of the windpipe, which leads into the lungs.

Food moves 1.1 inches (2.8 centimeters) in the small intestine every minute.

The small intestine is about 22 feet (6.7 meters) long, while the large intestine is 5 feet (1.5 meters) long. Most food is digested and absorbed into the body while in the small intestine. The food is moved through the small intestine by peristalsis. Peristalsis is a movement of the muscles in which alternating waves of contraction and relaxation cause the food to be squeezed along the digestive tract. The lining of the small intestine has millions of microscopic fingerlike projections called villi and microvilli, which absorb useful nutrients from digested food in the same way fibers on a bath towel absorb water. The total surface area of the small intestine is 718 square yards (600.3 square meters), which is about the size of a small tennis court.

Every minute, 1.5 quarts (1.4 liters) of blood travel through the liver.

The liver is the largest gland and internal organ in the human body. It only weighs 3.5 pounds (1.6 kilograms). The liver is roughly the size of a football and is located on the right side of the body right under the rib cage. The liver gets nutrient-rich blood directly from your small intestine. This is important so that the liver can detoxify any harmful substance you may have eaten. The liver is a huge chemical processing factory that performs more than 200 functions. Besides producing important chemicals needed for digestion, the liver also breaks down fats and produces cholesterol.

A sneeze travels about 100 miles (160.9 kilometers) per hour or 1.7 miles (2.7 kilometers) a minute. Knock, knock! Who is there? Hutch! Hutch who? Bless you, do you need a tissue? A sneeze is the nose's way of kicking out an unwanted guest. It is a reflex that is triggered when the nerve endings inside the mucous membrane of the nose are stimulated by an irritant. The irritant may be dust, pollen, chemicals, infection, or similar causes. Some people even sneeze when they are chilled, others when they pluck their eyebrows. Walking out into bright sunlight can cause some people to sneeze. It is called the photic sneeze reflex and affects about 25 percent of the population.

Activity 1

Heart Beater

Believe it or not, your heart is composed of a special type of muscle called cardiac muscle. It is special because, unlike your other muscles, it moves without you instructing it, like it is on autopilot. Every time your heart beats, more of your blood is being sent out to the rest of your body. Every time you stretch your arm or walk down stairs, you are constantly telling your body which muscles to move, how quickly, and in which direction. Could you imagine if you had to do the same for your heart? As soon as you went to sleep, it would stop beating! Even without your commands, it does a fine job monitoring just how much blood to pump. You can observe this for yourself. Take your pulse for one minute sitting still. Write that number down. Now, run in place for one minute and then count how many times your heart beats in a minute. What is the difference in beats? You can experiment by doing different activities—jumping rope, walking, doing sit-ups, jumping jacks, etc. Which activity increases your resting heart rate the most?

82

Activity 2

First Letter Frenzy

The human brain is one of the most powerful and fascinating objects on the planet; let's see what yours can do. In addition to memorizing and creating, your brain also allows you to categorize the world around you. In order to demonstrate this, take out a pencil and piece of paper. Now, if you were to write as many words as you could in a minute, your hand might never stop moving. However, for this activity, you are to write as many words as you can, one letter at a time. Set your timer for a minute and begin with the letter **A**. Write as many words as you can that start with **A**. When you are done, move on to **B**. Keep going until you make it through the entire alphabet. Which letter was your best? Which letter was the hardest? Once you think you've got it down, challenge a friend or family member. You can even take turns choosing which letter.

TECHNOLOGY

A car going 60 miles (96.5 kilometers) per hour can travel 1 mile (1.6 kilometers) or 5,280 feet (1,609.3 meters, or 17.6 football fields) in a minute. That breaks down into 88 feet (26.8 meters) per second. So if it takes a driver two seconds to react to an emergency and hit the brakes, the car will have traveled 176 feet (53.6 meters) or a little more than half the length of a football field before the brakes are applied. It could travel another 176 feet (53.6 meters) before coming to a stop. Many people are not aware of how far they are traveling every second and how long it takes to react to an emergency.

A commercial jet plane like the ones people travel on for vacation and business can travel 9.3 miles (15 kilometers) or 49,104 feet (14,967 meters) in a minute.

That means it goes about 560 miles (901 kilometers) per hour. Do you ever wonder why commercial jets fly at an altitude of more than 30,000 feet (9,144 meters)? It takes more time and fuel to get to that height, but the air is thinner at that altitude, about two times thinner than at sea level. Less air means the jet can travel with less resistance, so it can travel faster and use less fuel than if the air was thicker.

☼ TECHNOLOGY ☼

The French bullet train V150 just broke the speed record in April 2007 with a speed of 357.2 miles (574.9 kilometers) per hour. Most bullet trains cruise at 186 miles (299.3 kilometers) per hour. **At that speed, it can travel 3.1 miles (5 kilometers) or 16,368 feet (4,989 meters) in a minute.** Another way to look at that speed is that the train is going one mile in 18 seconds and 1 kilometer in 12 seconds. Japan started the bullet trains in 1964. At that time, the fastest train could travel 124 miles (199.5 kilometers) per hour. Today, Japan and France are competing to see who can build the fastest commercial train. The French held the record for some time with their TGV lines that traveled out from Paris to Belgium, the Netherlands, Germany, and the United Kingdom.

In one minute, 35mm movie film travels 90 feet (27.4 meters) through a theater film projector.

Have you ever wondered how long a two-hour movie is in feet (meters)? The two-hour (120-minute) movie times the 90 feet (27.4 meters) per minute gives a total distance of 10,800 feet (3,291.8 meters). That is a little more than two miles (3.2 kilometers).

The Indianapolis 500 is the oldest auto race in the world. The track was originally built for automotive research for cars, and then turned into a racetrack. During a race, Indy cars make 200 laps around the 2.5-mile (4-kilometer) track. The 3.5-liter methanol-powered engines of the Indy cars can produce 675 horsepower and revolve at a maximum rate of 10,300 revolutions per minute. When racing at over 200 miles (321.8 kilometers) per hour, Indy cars get less than 2 miles (3.2 kilometers) per gallon of fuel. These cars can accelerate from 0 to 100 miles (0 to 160.9 kilometers) per hour in less than 3 seconds!

The SR-71 spy (reconnaissance) plane, also known as the *Blackbird,* can go 36 miles (57.9 kilometers) in a minute, which is faster than the speed of a rifle bullet. The SR-71 can fly at speeds of over Mach 3.2 and at an altitude of 85,000 feet (25,908.1 meters). From a height of 80,000 feet (24,384 meters) it could spy on 100,000 square miles (256,400 square kilometers) of Earth in an hour. The SR-71 is currently retired after being brought into service in 1966. The SR-71 holds the absolute speed record of 2,193 miles (3,528.5 kilometers) per hour. One flew from coast to coast (California to Virginia) in 64 minutes. On September 1, 1974, an SR-71 traveled from New York to London in 1 hour and 54 minutes. It takes a Boeing 747 about 6 hours to make the same flight.

Every minute about 191 cell phones are discarded in the United States.

What happens to all the discarded phones? Some are donated to charities and others just sit around in people's homes. Many are thrown away and end up in landfills, creating a pollution problem. Consumers are getting new phones about every 16 months on average. Phone technology is changing rapidly, resulting in phones that have more and more features and style choices. The newer phones have the ability to take pictures and download and play music, music videos, and podcasts. The latest cell phones have GPS navigation capabilities that help people find their way in cities and on highways. Now it is even possible to view TV broadcasts using your cell phone.

An estimated 954 camera phones are sold worldwide every minute.

Around 500 million camera phones were sold worldwide in 2006. That number represents 38 percent of all the mobile phones sold. In 2004, camera phones only accounted for 14 percent of all mobile phone sales. By 2008, it is predicted that 70 percent of all mobile phones in the world will have a built-in camera. In 2006, camera phones with 3.2 megapixels were introduced. These camera phones can take very detailed photos, comparable to those taken by basic digital cameras. Camera phones are continually getting smaller and lighter, while offering a greater variety of features.

More than 186 digital cameras are sold in the United States every minute.

In 2006, 98 million digital cameras were sold worldwide. Digital cameras use electronic "film" instead of photographic film. Digital cameras have electronic sensors that are sensitive to light. The plates are composed of microscopic sections called pixels. Pixel is short for picture elements. The images taken with a digital camera are stored on a memory card as digital data. Scientists believe that photographs taken with 20-megapixel digital cameras of the future will be of a quality that is equal to today's photographic film.

An estimated 802 music CDs are purchased in the United States every minute. The letters *CD* stand for compact disc. Color photos and documents can also be stored on a **CD**. The information on a CD can be stored for 100 years without losing data. VCR tapes and floppy discs are not dependable after ten years. However, the number of CDs sold has been slipping ever since the year 2000. During that year 942.5 million CDs, worth $13.2 billion, were shipped. In 2004, the total number shipped was 767 million, and in 2005 the total number dropped to 705.4 million. The main reason **CD** sales have declined is because people are downloading music to their **MP3** players, computers, and now even cell phones.

More than 2,500 music downloads are purchased in the United States every minute. The total number of downloads was 139.4 million in 2004. That number then skyrocketed to 366.9 million in 2005. People are downloading music on the smaller MP3 players and giving up their bulky CD players. More than two million songs can be downloaded from music sites on the Internet. There are more than 350 legal music download sites in the world. Some MP3 players weigh only as much as two CDs and hold 10,000 songs, which translates to the ability to play songs 24/7 for four weeks. The 60-gig MP3 players can hold 10,000 songs, 25,000 photographs, and 150 minutes of streaming video.

The Philadelphia Mint, which is the world's largest mint, produces 15,427 coins each minute.

The United States has mints in Denver, San Francisco, and West Point. In 1792 at the original Philadelphia mint, a lone watchman armed with a sword, pistol, and watchdog was the only security. Harness horses were used to run the machinery at the mint. The mint's first coins were made of gold, silver, and copper. George and Martha Washington donated household silver to make the first coins. The mint's first delivery was 11,178 copper coins in 1793. The first coins with "In God We Trust" on them were minted between 1864 and 1873. By an Act of Congress on July 30, 1956, "In God We Trust" became the national motto of the United States.

TECHNOLOGY

A car uses 1.6 ounces (47.3 milliliters) of gasoline while idling for one minute. How much gasoline would Americans burn if all of their 240 million vehicles (cars, trucks, and SUVs) were just idling for one minute? Drum roll!!!! All those vehicles would be burning around 1.9 million gallons (7.2 million liters) of gasoline in that minute. That is a lot of gasoline, but if they were all zipping down the highway at 60 miles (96.5 kilometers) per hour, they would use four or five times as much. Something new on the scene is hybrid vehicles, which have two power sources, a standard gasoline engine and an electric motor with batteries. Some of the newer hybrid cars will shut off their gasoline engine when the car is idling at a stop sign, but will keep the electric motor running. There are also totally electric cars, which use no gasoline at all.

FUEL 2 MILES

98

The fastest escalator travels 98 feet (29.9 meters) per minute.

An escalator is a conveyor transport device consisting of moving steps that move people to a higher level. Most escalators work in pairs, one going up, and one going down. The world's longest uninterrupted escalator is at the Wheaton station of the Washington (D.C.) Metro system. It takes about 2 minutes and 45 seconds to travel up or down the 508-foot (154.8-meter) span. The Washington Metro system has four of the five longest escalators in the United States. The longest outdoor escalator system is Hong Kong's Central-Mid-Level. This system is 2,625 feet (800.1 meters) long and only goes in one direction but is reversed during afternoon rush hour.

The fastest supercomputer can execute 4.2 quadrillion instructions a minute.

One company has plans to build an even faster supercomputer for the U.S. Department of Energy's Oak Ridge Laboratory in Tennessee. The peak speed of that supercomputer will be 1 petaflop, which is one quadrillion calculations a second. In less than 30 seconds, the petaflop supercomputer would be able to process information equivalent to all 20 million volumes in the New York Public Library system. The United States has six of the fastest supercomputers in the world, followed by Japan with two, France with one, and Germany with one. Supercomputers are used by animated film companies to produce movies like *The Incredibles*, *Finding Nemo*, and *Toy Story*. Sony's newest PlayStation® (PS3) is capable of doing about 2 teraflops, or 2 billion calculations a second.

All over the world, three patent applications are made each minute, but only about 1 patent is granted each minute. The U.S. Patent and Trademark Office (USPTO) officials estimate that there are more than 50 million patents worldwide. The USPTO is located in Alexandria, Virginia, with a workforce of 7,100 employees. More than 3,000 employees are patent examiners, and 250 are trademark examiners. The USPTO has issued 7 million patents since it started in 1790. The IBM Corporation was issued the most patents, 2,941, in the year 2005. It was followed by Canon (Japan) with 1,828 patents and Hewlett-Packard with 1,797 patents. The IBM Corporation has lead in the number of patents granted for 13 years (as of 2005).

Can a jet plane climb faster than a rocket being launched? It depends on the jet plane and rocket. **An F-15 Eagle can climb straight up 30,000 feet (9,144 meters) in one minute.** A specially modified F-15 Eagle, called "Streak Eagle," was able to outclimb a Saturn V moon rocket to a distance of 60,000 feet (18,288 meters). The F-15 Eagle flew to 98,430 feet (30,001.5 meters) in 3 minutes and 30 seconds. The F-15 Eagle has two engines that produce a total of 50,000 pounds (22,727.3 kilograms) of thrust. A lightly loaded F-15 Eagle weighs 48,000 pounds (21,818.2 kilograms), so the total thrust is greater than the weight of the plane. The F-15 Eagle is the only airplane that can accelerate as it climbs; other planes either keep the same speed or slow down.

Tires are made at the rate of 572 a minute in the United States every year, which adds up to about 300 million tires. Some of the most interesting tires are the ones made for the Indianapolis (Indy) 500 race cars. The front tire only weighs 18 pounds (8.2 kilograms), the average size of a one-year-old child. During the race the temperature of the tires can reach over 200°F (93°C). The heat causes the tires to become tarlike, which helps the tires stick to the track. At the average speed of an Indy car, which is 220 miles (354 kilometers), the front tires can rotate at 43 times a second. During one lap, one of these tires will revolve 1,955 times, and in its 30-lap life it could revolve more than 60,000 times.

The Georgia Aquarium (the world's largest) has 218 pumps that filter 261,000 gallons (986,580 liters) of water a minute.

That's about 163,125 toilet flushes. All the tanks in the aquarium hold a total 8 million gallons (3.2 million liters) of water that is cleaned and recycled constantly. The aquarium holds more than 100,000 fish and other sea creatures. Sixty habitats house about 500 different species of fish. The largest tank, Ocean Voyager, holds 75 percent of the aquarium's water. The tank measures 263 feet long (80.2 meters) by 126 feet (38.4 meters) wide. It is a whopping 33 feet (10.1 meters) deep and holds 6 million gallons (22.7 million liters) of water!

The U.S. Bureau of Engraving and Printing is using 25 pounds (11.4 kilos) of ink to make 25,694 bills worth $483,333 each minute.

The first U.S. currency, or paper money, was issued in 1861. During the Civil War, the Bureau was called upon to print paper notes in the denominations of 3, 5, 10, 25, and 50 cents. The size of paper currency has shrunk from 3 by 7.4 inches (7.6 by 18.8 centimeters) to the current size of 2.6 by 6 inches (6.6 by 15.2 centimeters). Paper money is not actually paper. It is made of 75 percent cotton and 25 percent linen, making it very tough. It would take 4,000 double folds (back and forth) to tear a dollar bill. The average life of a dollar bill is 22 months. A $10 bill lasts only 18 months, while a $100 bill lasts five years.

Activity 1

Court Reporter

Court reporters can type from 225 to 300 words per minute on their steno machines. While a steno machine may make typing easier, it is still quite a challenge. Whether you use it to become a better student, create an attractive blog, or advance in your career, typing is an extremely useful skill for just about everyone. Now is your chance to practice. Grab a newspaper and your timer. Open the newspaper up to an article and see how much of it you can type in a minute on your computer. Count your words and mistakes. Do you think you are ready to become a court reporter yet? Next, turn on a television or radio next to your computer and try typing a conversation between two or more people. Could you keep up with them for a minute? If you don't have a computer, you can grab a pencil and paper and write the words down instead.

Activity 2

Build a House

Have you ever built a house of cards? It takes more than a steady hand; it takes careful planning. Your challenge is to build a house of cards but, just like house builders in real life, you have a deadline. In this case, your deadline is one minute. How high can you build your house? Try challenging someone else to build alongside of you. After you compete according to height, see who can use the most number of cards in their house. Remember, the more cards you use, the heavier your house becomes. Where should that extra weight go so your house doesn't come tumbling down?

A honeybee's wings beat 75,000 times a minute, too fast for the human eye to see clearly; all you see is a blur. It would take a camera with a shutter speed of 0.0005 of a second to stop the motion of the bee's wing movement. The bee's wings are small in comparison to its body, so they have to move rapidly in order to keep the bee's body aloft. By comparison, a housefly's wing beat is 11,400 times a minute. Since a housefly does not have to hover like a honeybee, it has a lower wing beat. The bumblebee has a wing beat of 7,800 times a minute. The bumblebee's wings are large, but so is its body. Aircraft engineers are amazed that bumblebees can even get off the ground, let alone fly.

A honeybee can travel 502 feet (153 meters) in a minute.

The worker honeybee goes through stages in its life. It is born as a worker and stays around the hive and cleans up. It helps build the comb with wax its body produces. Later, it learns how to fly and stays around the front of the hive as a guard bee. Finally, it graduates to a forager. The forager honeybee has to collect nectar and pollen from flowers for the survival of the bee colony in the beehive. They travel great distances compared to their size to visit the blooming flowers. Most flowers open in the early morning and produce a limited supply of nectar, so the early bees get the nectar. This means the honeybees must travel quickly to get the available nectar.

A garden snail can move 0.31 inches (7.8 millimeters) a minute.

Have you ever seen a trail of slime on the ground? A snail probably made it. A land snail produces slime from its "stomach foot," which it uses to move. The snail lays down a slime that allows it to travel across many different kinds of surfaces without injuring this foot. One reason the snail moves so slowly is that it is paving the road it travels on with its own pavement (slime). The fastest snail is the speckled garden snail; it can travel 55 yards (50.3 meters) in an hour. That is a "blazing" 33 inches (83.8 centimeters) a minute. Some snails can lift seven times their body weight on a vertical surface. The largest land snail is the giant African land snail, which can weigh 2 pounds (909 grams) and measure 15.5 inches (39.4 centimeters) from head to back of foot.

A sloth can travel 13 feet (4 meters) in one minute.

Most people believe that the sloth is lazy, but scientists believe that moving slowly helps protect it from predators. Sloths live in the tropical rain forest in South America. They move so slowly that green algae grows on their fur. This also helps hide them from predators. Sloths eat, sleep, mate, and even give birth upside down. Their hair curves up from their stomach to their back. Sloths feed on leaves, young shoots, and buds, taking up to a month to digest a meal. There are two species of sloths; the two-toed and the three-toed both have long and extremely sharp claws on their toes. Interestingly, even though sloths cannot walk well, they are very good swimmers.

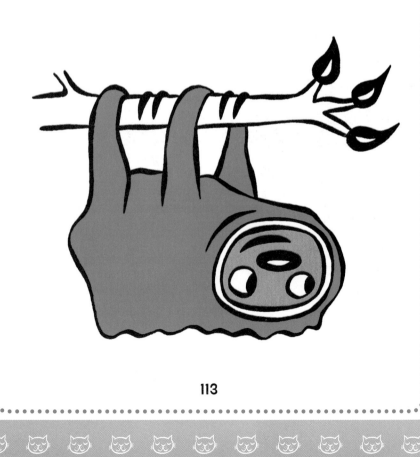

Do you think you can outrun a giant tortoise? Well, I hope so. **A giant tortoise can walk 15 feet (4.6 meters) a minute.** See how far you can walk in a minute. During the National Tortoise Championship in Tickhill, South Yorkshire, United Kingdom, the record run was timed at 24.6 feet (7.5 meters) a minute. By the way, turtles live in water and tortoises live on land. Giant tortoises live on the Galapagos Islands off the coast of Ecuador. The adults have very few predators so they do not need to move very fast. The oldest known giant tortoise was named Harriet. She lived to be 175 years old. That is 91,728,000 minutes. Harriet died on June 26, 2006, at the Australia Zoo in Beerwah, Queensland. Other giant tortoises can be protected by supporting the Tortoise Trust and the Galapagos Conservation Trust.

A squid can speed up to 2,187 feet (666.6 meters) in a minute. The squid

is really a "jet" in disguise. It uses a propulsion system to move through the water. The squid takes water into a special chamber and then, by contracting its muscles, forces the water out another opening, propelling itself backward. Squids need to be able to move quickly for they are the favorite food of many ocean predators. The squid can move more than 364 feet (110.9 meters) in less than ten seconds, which is faster than Olympic runners can run. When threatened, a squid can squirt ink to create a pseudomorph, or "false body" in the water that a predator may go after instead of the squid.

Interesting Facts:

• The giant squid can be 60 feet (18.3 meters) long and weigh 1,980 pounds (900 kilograms).

• The giant squid's eyes are the size of basketballs, making them the largest eyes in the animal kingdom.

A cheetah can run 1.2 miles (1.9 kilometers) or 6,336 feet (1,931.2 meters) in one minute.

It can accelerate faster than any land animal and most sports cars. It can go from a standstill to 50 miles (113 kilometers) per hour in three seconds. The cheetah can maintain this speed for only 400 yards (365.8 meters), though. When a cheetah is running at full speed, only one foot at a time is touching the ground, and its stride covers 25 feet (7.6 meters). The name cheetah comes from the Indian word for "spotted one." Unlike other spotted cats, the cheetah has long, dark teardrop lines on each side of its nose from its eyes to the corners of its mouth. These lines keep the glare of the sun out of its eyes, which helps in hunting.

Can you imagine tunneling three times your body length underground? That's what earthworms do. **Earthworms can tunnel underground 10.8 inches (27.4 centimeters) in a minute.** They do the tunneling without tools. They just use their head and body. Earthworms eat some of the soil as they burrow through it, deriving nutrition from organic matter like decaying roots and leaves. They also eat other living organisms like fungi and bacteria. They can consume one-third of their body weight each day. In an acre (0.4 hectare) of soil, there can be more than a million earthworms that can eat 10 tons (9.1 metric tons) of decaying and living things a year. The largest earthworm ever captured was 22 feet (6.7 meters) long, and was found in South Africa.

The queen bee is an egg-laying factory, laying more than one egg a minute.

There is only one queen to a hive. The worker bees bring her food called royal jelly, which is made by special cells in the bodies of the young workers. All the queen does is lay eggs around the clock. Queen bees can live up to five years. Drones live only four to six weeks, while worker bees live five to six weeks during the active working season, but several months during the winter. Honeybees are unusual insects because they have both chewing and sucking mouthparts, while most insects have only one or the other. They use sucking mouthparts to gather honey and chewing mouthparts to chew wax to mend the hive.

Rat-a-tat-tat, rat-a-tat-tat goes the woodpecker as it hammers its bill into the tree trunk looking for insects hidden under or in the bark. **A woodpecker can hammer with its bill 150 times a minute.** Sometimes the woodpecker drills a larger hole in the tree in which it will make a nest for shelter and raising its young. There are 215 species of woodpeckers found in locations ranging from tundra areas in North America to the tip of South America. Woodpeckers have the longest tongues of all birds, extending as much as 2 inches (5.1 centimeters) past their bill. Several species of woodpeckers have salivary glands that produce sticky saliva that coats the tongue, helping it capture insects.

A migrating monarch butterfly can fly almost 1,000 feet (304.8 meters) a minute.

In the fall of the year, the monarch butterfly migrates more than 1,000 miles (1,609 kilometers) to points in the United States and Mexico to winter in the warmer climate. The monarchs are poisonous to animals that might eat them. When in the larva (caterpillar) stage, they feed only on the milkweed plant, which contains chemicals that are poisonous. These chemicals remain in the monarch's body for the rest of its life. There is even a butterfly called the viceroy that mimics the wing color and pattern of the monarch to protect it from predators, but the viceroy is not poisonous.

Boing! Boing! Boing! There goes the animal kingdom's answer to a pogo stick, the kangaroo. **The fastest kangaroo can go 0.7 mile (1.1 kilometers) in a minute, or about 40 miles (64.3 kilometers) per hour.**
The kangaroo's legs act like springs. A popular legend tells us that when the first Europeans saw the kangaroo, they asked the Aborigines (native Australians) what they called the animal. A man replied, "Kangaroo." He meant, "I don't understand your question." The explorers thought this was the animal's name, and that is what it has been called ever since. The male kangaroo is called a boomer, the female is called a flyer, and the baby is a joey.

More than 5,500 animal species are threatened with extinction every minute.

It is hard to believe that in today's world of computers and other technology more than 5,000 animal species live with the daily threat of extinction. Many of the habitats of the threatened animals are being destroyed at an alarming rate. Without a place to live, threatened animals move to other nearby places. However, if the new places do not have proper food, water, shelter, space, and other necessities, the animals will not be able to survive. Some good news is that there are more than 3,500 protected areas in the world. These areas are national and state parks, wildlife refuges, and wildlife reserves.

More plant species face extinction than animal species. **More than 34,000 plant species are threatened with extinction each minute.** Plants cannot run and hide like animals and are easily destroyed by the machinery and chemicals of man. It is estimated that thousands of plant species have yet to be discovered by botanists. Some plant species no doubt have faced extinction even before being discovered by botanists. An endangered species is in immediate danger of becoming extinct. An advantage plant species have over animal species is that plant seeds can be stored in seed banks, places where seeds are stored in controlled environments. Currently, there are seeds of more than 6 million different plant species stored at 1,300 sites around the world. However, most of these seeds are for crops people grow. Only 15 percent of the seeds stored are for wild plant species.

Many people in the world depend on smaller fish to provide food for them. **About 43 tons (39.1 metric tons) of herring, sardines, and anchovies are being caught in fishing nets every minute.** Herring, sardines, and anchovies are sometimes eaten whole, head, skin, fins, and all. Herring is the common name for many a marine and freshwater fish. There are so many different kinds of small fish in the world that instead of naming them all, the general name of herring is used. Herring are small fish but very plentiful. They travel in schools and feed on plankton and small animals. Herring are a vital link in the food chain because many larger animals depend on them as a food source.

Silkworms are producing 143 pounds (65 kilograms) of silk a minute.

Silk is one of the strongest fibers known to humans, and can be made into some of the softest and smoothest garments. The silkworm larva needs 2,200 pounds (1,000 kilograms) of mulberry leaves to produce 11 pounds (5 kilograms) of silk. The silkworm will spend three to five days spinning its cocoon. It will stay in the cocoon for about two weeks and hatch out as a moth. The silkworm moths do not eat, drink, or fly and only live for five days. During that time the moths mate and the female lays between 300 and 500 eggs, each the size of a pinhead.

Interesting Facts:

• It takes 600 silkworm cocoons to make a silk tie.
• It takes 2,000 cocoons to make a silk dress.

The hummingbird gets its name from the humming sound its wings make when it is flying. Hummingbirds are able to fly right, left, up, down, forward, backward, and even upside down. These tiny birds are able to hover by flapping their wings in figure eight patterns. Their wings are made of bones, like in your hands, instead of arm bones like most birds, which make them more maneuverable.

The resting heart rate of most hummingbirds is 50 to 180 beats a minute. The blue-throated hummingbird's wings beat fastest, at 1,260 beats per minute when it's flying.

Interesting Facts:

- The hummingbird's long tongue can lick nectar 13 times a second.
- Hummingbirds are called nectivores because 90 percent of their food is nectar.
- Hummingbirds can digest a fruit fly in ten minutes.
- Hummingbird eggs are the size of a coffee bean (smaller species).
- Hummingbirds like to take baths.
- Hummingbirds have good memories, so keep feeders filled.

Sailfish are believed to be the fastest fish species in the world. It has been clocked at speeds greater than 68 miles (109.4 kilometers) per hour. The sailfish travels 1.1 miles (1.7 kilometers) a minute, or 6,000 feet (1828.8 meters) a minute at top speed. It feeds on fish like mackerel, sardines, and anchovies. When it sees a school of prey, it folds its saillike dorsal fin down halfway and starts swimming at half speed. As the sailfish gets within striking range, it folds its sail down completely and goes full speed ahead. The sailfish strikes the fish with its bill, which either kills or stuns them, so it can eat them. Sailfish can grow up to 11 feet (3.4 meters) and weigh 200 pounds (90.9 kilograms). They are found in the Pacific, Atlantic, and Indian Oceans.

A white-throated spine-tailed swift can fly 1.75 miles (2.8 kilometers), or 9,240 feet (2,816.4 meters), in a minute.

This bird, also known as needle-tailed swift or spine-tailed swift, is the fastest-flying bird in level, flapping wing flight, being capable of 106 miles (170.6 kilometers) per hour. The swift does spend most of its time in the air catching insects to eat. Swifts feed on flying insects like termites, ants, beetles, and flies. Swifts can even drink water in flight. The swifts live in central Asia and southern Siberia. In the winter, they migrate to Australia. They often occur in large numbers over northern and eastern Australia.

The hibernating American black bear's heartbeat is 8 beats per minute.

The American black bear is one of eight kinds of bears: polar bear, giant panda bear, Asiatic black bear, sloth bear, spectacled bear, sun bear, and brown bear, better known as the grizzly bear. Bears live on all continents except Africa, Australia, and Antarctica. Yes, there are no polar bears at the South Pole. The South Pole has penguins and the North Pole has polar bears. Black bears that live in western states are often different shades of brown. Black bears can have a blue and even white color phase in certain regions of British Columbia and Alaska.

Interesting Facts:

- Black bears can eat 45 pounds (20.5 kilograms) of food a day; their diet is 98 percent plants.
- Black bears can live about 18 to 20 years.
- Black bears can run faster than most humans.
- Black bears have a super sense of smell.
- Black bears do not urinate or defecate while hibernating.

An average basking shark could filter enough seawater to fill a swimming pool in one hour. **More than 1,111 gallons (4,199.6 liters) of water are being pulled by the gills of a basking shark in a minute.** The basking shark is the second largest fish in the world. Only the whale shark is larger. Their average length is 28.5 feet (8.7 meters), but the longest one ever observed was 45 feet (13.7 meters). That is longer than a bus. They can weigh 7 tons (6.4 metric tons), as much as two elephants. Even a newborn basking shark is huge, measuring 5 to 6.5 feet (1.5 to 2 meters) long. And the mother shark usually has six pups at a time! Basking sharks are not aggressive and pose no threat to people. They can be seen off the coast of New Brunswick and Nova Scotia, Canada.

How much can a whale inhale?

In a minute, 15,000 gallons (56,724 liters) of air are inhaled by a blue whale. How does a whale

breathe when it is sleeping? Scientists believe that only half of the whale brain sleeps; the other half stays awake. When the blue whale exhales, the air comes out at 300 miles (482.7 kilometers) per hour. The resulting blow or spout can be 32.8 feet (10 meters) high and 22 to 25 feet (6.7 to 7.6 meters) wide and can be seen for several miles (kilometers). The blue whale can empty 90 percent of its lungs in two seconds. They inhale 1,188 gallons (4,490.6 liters) of fresh air with each breath, which is 90 percent of their lung capacity. Most land animals, including humans, only inhale 10 to 20 percent of their lung capacity.

Interesting Facts:

- A blue whale uses 3 million calories a day.
- Blue whales can be 100 feet (30.4 meters) long.
- Whales have two blowholes, and dolphins only have one.
- A baby blue whale can gain 200 pounds (90.9 kilograms) a day.

131

Ten adult elephants can produce 1 pound (0.5 kilogram) of poop per minute.

Elephants are big eaters and not all of the food they eat is digested, so it is eliminated out the other end as poop. At the National Zoo in Washington, D.C., the elephants are fed 125 pounds (56.8 kilograms) of hay, 10 pounds (4.5 kilograms) of herbivore pellets, 10 pounds (4.5 kilograms) of vegetables and fruit, and a few leafy branches every day. You would eat that much, too, if you weighed 14,000 pounds (6363.6 kilograms), stood 11 feet (3.4 meters) tall, and were 25 feet (7.6 meters) long. That is the size of the largest African elephant, which is the largest land animal. Elephants are the only animals with a trunk, which is made of the nose and upper lip. The trunk allows the elephant to reach the ground, pick up things, tear down things, and squirt water in its mouth and on its body and blow dust on its back.

Dolphins click out 60,000 ultrasound waves a minute.

The dolphins use these clicks to locate food, communicate with other dolphins, and find the size and nature of surrounding objects. Dolphins can make an enormous variety of sounds, since they produce sounds in ranges that are 10 times higher pitched than humans can hear. Bottlenose dolphins have keen vision both in water and air, but they have no sense of smell.

Interesting Facts:

- Bottlenose dolphins can measure 13 feet (4 meters) and weigh 600 pounds (272.7 kilograms).
- Bottlenose dolphins live in tropical waters and stay within 100 miles (160.9 kilometers) of the shore.

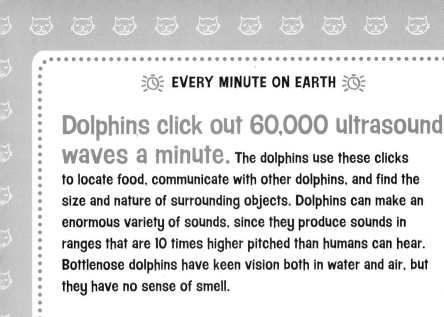

Americans buy $28,617 worth of pet food every minute. It takes that much
food because there are 60 million pet dogs and 75 million pet cats in the United States. The cat population overtook the dog population in 1987. A survey in 2002 showed that 36 percent of American households had one or more dogs and nearly 34 percent had at least one cat in their home. Americans spend more money on cat food than on baby food. Today there are nearly 100 different breeds of the domestic cat. Dogs beat cats in the number of breeds; there are 701 types of pure breed dogs and a gazillion types of mixed breeds. Designed dogs are the newest trend. They include the labradoodle and the puggle.

About 134 horses are born every minute. One out of every seven horses is found in China. The world's horse population is estimated to be around 75 million. That number is equal to the people living in the Philippines or Vietnam. There are more than 350 different breeds of horses and ponies in the world. The groups are light horses like the Thoroughbred and Arabian; the heavy or draft horses such as the Clydesdale and shire; the ponies, which are less than 58 inches (1.5 meters) tall, like the Shetland and Caspian; and the feral or wild horses such as the mustangs in the western United States.

Interesting Facts:

- A horse cannot breathe through its mouth.
- The horse is the state animal of New Jersey.
- A horse can see in two directions at the same time.
- During a race, a racehorse will lose 15 to 20 pounds (6.8 to 9.1 kilograms).
- Horses can make the following eight sounds: snort, squeal, roar, blow, neigh, greeting nicker, maternal nicker, and courtship nicker.

Large swarms of desert locusts can eat 27,778 pounds (12,626.4 kilograms) of grain and plants in a minute. The desert locusts live in arid deserts of Africa, the Near East, and southern and western Asia during quiet periods. This is an area of 11.3 million square miles (16 million square kilometers) consisting of 30 countries. The locust can actually develop a swarming behavior. The green ones change into black-and-yellow coloration and act as a group instead of individual insects. The adult locust can eat its body weight in food every day. A swarm can travel as far as 62 miles (99.8 kilometers) a day and 2,175 miles (3,660.1 kilometers) a month. Consider this: 1.1 tons (1 metric ton) of locusts can eat as much food as 10 elephants or 2,500 people. A swarm of desert locusts can eat all the green vegetation in an area in less than an hour.

Do you think babies slobber a lot? Dairy cows can produce 4.2 ounces (124.2 milliliters) of saliva every minute.
Talk about a slow eater—a cow can spend up to eight hours a day chewing its food. What is gross is the cow will regurgitate its food and chew it again; this helps the cow digest. Cows can consume 100 pounds (45.5 kilograms) of feed and 20 pounds (9.1 kilograms) of grain and drink a bathtub full of water a day. During their day, cows can produce 200 pounds (90.9 kilograms) of flatulence and burps a day. How do you weigh flatulence?

Interesting Facts:

• A cow has four stomachs.
• A dairy cow can produce 60 pounds (27.3 kilograms) of milk a day.
• A cow spends 13 hours lying down.

Activity 1

Bug Hunt

Nobody wants to find a bunch of bugs living in their home; they don't pay rent! What about outside, though? After all, the outdoors is a bug's natural home. But how many bugs are there exactly, sharing that home? Your challenge is to go outside, a park or your backyard is fine. Give yourself one minute to dig through the ground, search trees, and scan the air for as many bugs as you can find. How many did you find? Can you find more than your friends? Too easy? If you need a greater challenge, see how many bugs you can catch in a minute. You can use a butterfly net or a jar with a lid to catch the bugs. When you are done, count them up. Also, for bonus points, count how many different types of bugs you caught. Remember to let the bugs go free once you are finished with the game.

Activity 2

Animal Name-Chain Game

Here is another fun way to challenge a friend in a test of animal knowledge. Each of you writes the name of an animal on a piece of paper and hands it to the other. Start your timer. Now, you both have one minute to make a name-chain out of the animal you have written on your piece of paper. How do you make a name-chain? Easy. Quickly look at the last letter of the animal. Now, think of another animal that begins with that letter. After you write your new animal, keep the chain going by writing another animal that begins with the final letter of your previous one. For example, if you have *elephant* on your paper, your chain might look something like this: *elephantigeratickangaroostrich* (or, elephant, tiger, rat, tick, kangaroo, ostrich). Whoever has the longest chain, wins.

FOOD

Nearly 130 tons (118.2 metric tons) of bananas are being harvested or eaten every minute.

Bananas are harvested every day of the year. The origin of the banana can be traced back to the jungles of Malaysia in Southeast Asia. Today, the largest producer of bananas is India, which produces more than 16 million tons (14.5 metric tons). There are more than 500 varieties of bananas worldwide. The highest rate of consumption is in East Africa's Uganda, where the consumption is 992 pounds (450.9 kilograms) per person per year. The average American eats more than 28 pounds (12.7 kilograms) of bananas each year. The banana plant is not grown from seeds but from cuttings from a mature banana plant. The banana plant is not considered a tree but an herb because of the structure of its stem.

Each minute, 1,145 tons (1,051.2 metric tons) of rice is being produced. Rice is one of the most eaten grains worldwide. Rice is the staple of 70 percent of the world's population. Rice originated in Asia and spread to other parts of the world. Rice was introduced to America by accident in 1694. There was a sailing vessel on its way from Madagascar to Europe that got caught in a storm and ended up in South Carolina. The colonists helped repair the ship, and the captain gave the colonists some rice. The rice grew so well that they had enough for themselves and traded the surplus. In tropical regions around the world, rice can be grown and harvested two to three times a year. Rice is a very healthy food and easy to digest.

Every minute, 10,268 pounds (4,667.3 kilograms) of tea are being produced.

The most consumed beverage in the world today after water is tea. Tea is made from the leaves of the tea plant. The three kinds of tea are green, black, and oolong. Green tea is made by immediately applying heat to the fresh picked leaves and then drying them. Black tea is made by tearing the fresh-picked leaves and exposing them to the air. This creates a chemical reaction in the leaves that produces the black color. Oolong is a cross between green and black tea. India is the largest tea producer in the world. One pound (454.5 grams) of tea can make 180 cups (42.5 liters) of brewed tea.

In one minute, 21,000 pizzas are baked.

The word pizza dates back to the 16th century, and the ingredients vary from country to country—peach slices and corn (Taiwan), sweet potato puree (South Korea), scrambled eggs and squid ink (Japan), and French fries fried together with the pizza (Scotland). The traditional toppings are tomatoes, mozzarella cheese, and basil. Regardless of what is put on top of it, it continues to conquer the world as one of the most popular foods.

Interesting Facts:

• October is National Pizza Month in the United States.

• In the United States alone, 3 billion pizzas are sold every year.

• The average American citizen eats 23 pounds (10.5 kilograms) of pizza (about 46 slices) every year.

• Americans are eating 350 slices of pizza every second. That is 2,100 every minute!

• Quick! How many pizzas do you think you have eaten in your life? One hundred? One thousand? Ten thousand? How about 259,000? Ross Taylor, the world record holder for most pizzas eaten in a lifetime, has eaten more than 259,000 pizzas in 21 years.

Every minute, 2,137 pounds (971.4 kilograms) of popcorn are being eaten. While most of that popcorn is coming from one state, Indiana, no fewer than *four* different cities—Ridgeway, Illinois; North Loup, Nebraska; Marion, Ohio; and Schaller, Iowa—all claim to be: "The Popcorn Capital of the World." In addition to four capital cities, there are more than ten different words for popcorn in Spanish, *palomitas de maiz*, depending on the country. Heck, people even seem to have trouble figuring out what to do with the little kernels. When Christopher Columbus first saw popcorn in the 15th century, the Native Americans were wearing it; French explorers in the 17th century found the Iroquois enjoying popcorn in soup; and the early American colonists ate it like breakfast cereal with cream and sugar.

In the United States, 18,315 pounds (8,325 kilograms) of food is being thrown away every minute. That comes out to about 25 percent of all of the food bought and grown in the country. But it is a small amount compared to the amount of food Great Britain throws away every year. The British lead the entire world in food waste. As a country, they throw out between 30 to 40 percent of their food. Just how much food is that? It is estimated that all of the edible food thrown out in Great Britain could feed more than 250,000 people!

147

Americans are wolfing down 16,666 hot dogs a minute; and between Memorial Day and Labor Day (also known as Hot Dog Season), the number jumps to 49,080 every minute.

In that same minute, world champion eater Takeru Kobayashi can eat 4.5 hot dogs all on his own! Legendary baseball slugger Babe Ruth is said to have eaten 24 hot dogs between games of a doubleheader, but he had more than a minute. What better place to eat a hot dog than a baseball park? Did you know that 9 percent of all hot dogs eaten in the United States are eaten at ballparks? This year, the number of hot dogs Americans will eat at major league baseball parks will be enough to stretch from San Francisco to Washington, D.C.—that is 2,800 miles (4505.2 km) of hot dogs!

Americans are eating 173 lobsters every minute, on average.

Around 63 million tons (57.3 metric tons) of lobsters are caught in the United States every year. Canadian provinces bring in 94 million pounds (42.7 million kilograms). Lobsters are crustaceans and are related to shrimp, crabs, crayfish, and barnacles. It is commonly believed that lobsters are scavengers but, in fact, lobsters catch fresh food like fish, crabs, clams, and sometimes other lobsters.

Interesting Facts:

- Lobsters have teeth in their stomachs. The lobster's stomach is very close to the mouth, and it has three grinding surfaces that look like molars.
- Most lobsters are greenish-brown, but rare ones can be colored blue, yellow, red, or white.
- The largest lobster ever caught measured 36 inches (91.4 centimeters) and weighed 42 pounds (19.1 kilograms).

149

Americans are drinking 208,333 cups of coffee every minute—but it is only grown in one of the 50 states—Hawaii.

There is so much to say about such a little bean! Did you know:

After petroleum, coffee is the most traded product in the world.

The average person spends 45 hours a year waiting in line to buy coffee on his or her way to work.

Interesting Facts:

- Brazil produces 30 to 40 percent of the world's coffee.
- Coffee is grown in more than 53 countries, but they are all located between the tropics of Cancer and Capricorn.

- On average, one coffee tree yields 1 pound (0.5 kilogram) of roasted coffee.
- Each year about 7 million tons (6.4 million metric tons) of green coffee beans are picked.

RISE AND SHINE

Valentine candy conversation hearts are produced at the rate of 15,263 a minute.

The company that makes them does so for 11 months out of the year, even though their peak selling period is only six weeks long. Guess when that is?

How long have lovers been conversing with candy? How about since the 18th century! Scratching love messages onto homemade candies was a popular activity of American colonists. In the mid-1800s, the New England Confectionary Company (NECCO) decided to capitalize on this practice and began mass production of the conversation hearts. However, at first, the candies were made into more than hearts—horseshoes and baseballs were also popular items. These shapes allowed for much longer messages than you read today. Sweethearts could even swap full-sentenced candies. Today, the hearts carry much shorter messages and they are updated regularly.

During the month of January, 6,000 cans of Campbell's Soup are sold every minute.

The Campbell's Soup Company was founded in 1869 by a fruit merchant and an icebox manufacturer. The company originally produced canned tomatoes, vegetables, jellies, soups, and condiments. The company hired a gifted chemist, Dr. John T. Dorrance, who developed a way for condensing soup by halving the amount of water in it. Campbell's condensed soup was entered at the Paris Exhibition in 1900 and won the gold medal, an image of which still appears on the label. The label's red-and-white color scheme was adopted in 1898 when proposed by an executive who liked the red and white colors of Cornell University's football team. The three top selling soups are Chicken Noodle, Cream of Mushroom, and Tomato. Consumers purchase almost 2.5 billion cans every year.

About 4,140 Oscar Mayer bologna sandwiches are eaten each minute.

This highly seasoned sausage gets its name from Bologna, Italy. However, the real Italian sausage from Bologna is actually called "mortadella." Mortadella is a very large smoked pork sausage containing cubes of pork fat, peppercorns, and pistachios. Americans eat more than 800 million pounds of bologna a year. Oscar Mayer makes five different kinds of bologna. They are Meat Bologna, Light Meat Bologna, Beef Bologna, Light Beef Bologna, Fat-Free Bologna, and Turkey Bologna. The company also makes hot dogs, bacon, and a variety of cold cuts.

Jars of Skippy peanut butter are sold at the rate of 180 a minute. That

is almost 90 million jars of peanut butter a year. Peanut butter was unique to America until the 1960s; most of the world had no idea of what it was. On average, Americans eat 3 pounds (1.4 kilograms) of peanut butter a year for a total of about 500 million pounds (227.3 million kilograms) a year. That much peanut butter could be spread over the entire floor of the Grand Canyon. Peanut butter was developed by a Saint Louis, Missouri, doctor for his patients with bad teeth. In 1933, a California packer homogenized the peanuts into butter and called it "Skippy Churned Peanut Butter."

Interesting Facts:

- Arachibutyrophobia is the fear of peanut butter sticking to the roof of your mouth.
- It takes about 540 peanuts to make a 12-ounce (341-gram) jar of peanut butter.

Kraft singles (cheese slices) are eaten at the rate of 7,740 slices a minute.

Cheese has been a popular food for more than 4,000 years. How do we know? What appear to be the remains of cheese have been found in ancient Egyptian tombs that old. Cheese was also popular in ancient Greece and Rome. Americans consume more than 8.8 billion pounds (4 billion kilograms) a year, which is 30.6 pounds (13.9 kilograms) per capita. Nearly 90 percent of all cheeses sold in the United States are classified as cheddar. However, the most popular cheese in America is mozzarella. Americans ate 2.8 billion pounds (1.3 billion kilograms) and most of it was on pizzas. There are more than 2,000 different kinds of cheese.

Krispy Kreme doughnuts are produced at the rate of 5,208 doughnuts a minute. That totals 2.7 billion a year. A typical Krispy Kreme store can produce 3,000 doughnuts an hour, but the larger ones can make 12,000 of the "gems" each hour. Who invented the doughnut? Archaeologists have discovered petrified fry cakes with holes in the center in Native American ruins in the southwestern United States. The Pennsylvania Dutch had cakes with nuts in the center and early settlers combined "dough" and "nuts" to make doughnuts. The New England sea captain Hanson Gregory punched a hole in the dough because his mother's doughnuts were not cooked in the center. You will never find doughnut holes at a Krispy Kreme because the machinery uses air pressure to extrude the doughnut from the dough to make a perfectly formed doughnut.

Americans are consuming 286,172 gallons (1,081,730.1 liters) of soda a minute.

The average teenage boy will drink two 12-ounce (354 milliliter) sodas per day, or more than 700 cans a year. The average teenage girl will drink 1.4 12-ounce (354 milliliter) sodas a day, or about 500 cans a year. More than 15 billion gallons (56.7 billion liters) of soda were sold to all age groups in the United States in 2000. In 2005, Americans drank around 54.3 gallons (206 liters) of soda per person per year. That is a gallon of soda a week. At one time, 60 percent of all public and private middle and high schools had soda machines. There is currently a move to replace all of these soda machines with fruit juice or flavored milk machines. Americans can choose between 450 different kinds of soft drinks.

Jack in the Box restaurants sell 600 tacos a minute.

That is a total of more than 315 million tacos a year. Jack in the Box was the very first fast food restaurant chain to have tacos on the menu at all of its restaurants. The chain uses 16 million tons (14.5 million metric tons) of fresh, stone-ground, U.S.-grown corn each year to make its tortillas. Along with the tacos, Jack in the Box gives out 136 million packets of taco sauce every year. Just for the tacos alone, Jack in the Box has to buy 11 million pounds (5 million kilograms) of beef each year. If placed end to end, the number of tacos Jack in the Box sells each year would stretch a distance of 28,500 miles (45,856.5 kilometers), which is more than once around the world's equator.

Every minute, 20,820 Jelly Belly jellybeans are produced.

Jellybeans were first made during the 1800s by an unknown candy maker. Jelly Belly beans were invented in 1976, and the original flavors were Very Cherry, Root Beer, Cream Soda, Tangerine, Green Apple, Lemon, Licorice, and Grape. Jelly Belly beans are different from other jellybeans because the natural flavors are inside the bean as well as in the shell. Other jellybeans just have flavor in the shell. President Ronald Reagan was a big fan of Jelly Belly. The blueberry flavor was created for President Reagan's inauguration in 1981 so red, white, and blue Jelly Belly beans could be eaten. More than 3 tons (2.7 metric tons) of Jelly Belly were consumed during the celebrations. There is even a portrait of President Reagan made from 10,000 Jelly Belly beans that hangs in his presidential library in Simi Valley, California.

Each minute, 17,000 candy corns are manufactured.

Candy manufacturers sold more than 20 million pounds (9 million kilograms) of candy corn from 2000-2006. That is an estimated guess of 8.3 billion kernels of candy corn. Candy corn is the tricolor candy that is so popular around Halloween. Candy corn has been around since 1898, when Gustav Goelitz began production in Cincinnati, Ohio. And it has remained practically unchanged since its creation. In the beginning, workers made three passes over a cornstarch-lined candy corn mold to make the tricolor corn. Nowadays, the processes are done by machines.

Approximately 5,723 Pez candies are made each minute.

Where did the name Pez come from, you may ask? It comes from the German word for peppermint, *pfefferminz*. If you take the first, middle, and last letter of the word, and put them together, you get Pez. Pez was invented in Vienna, Austria, by candy maker Edward Haas III during the 1920s. The original purpose of the Pez candy was as a breath mint for cigarette smokers. The first Pez dispenser arrived in 1947 and looked like a cigarette lighter. In 1952, the first fruit-flavored Pez was marketed with the first Pez dispensers with character heads on them.

Interesting Facts:

- The first flavors were cherry, lemon, orange, and strawberry.
- The best selling dispensers are Mickey Mouse, Santa, and Dino the dinosaur.
- There have been more than 275 character heads on the dispensers.
- Before 1987, Pez dispensers did not have feet, but now they do.
- Anyone who collects Pez dispensers is called a Pezhead.

161

Exactly 55,555 Hershey's KISSES are produced every minute.

Hershey makes around 80 million Hershey's KISSES at their Hershey, Pennsylvania, and California plants every day. Hershey's KISSES were first introduced in 1907. Some people think that Hershey's KISSES may have gotten their name from the machine that makes the candy. The machine looks and sounds like it is "kissing" the conveyor belt when it deposits the soft chocolate. The first Hershey's KISSES had to be wrapped by hand, but now machines can wrap 1,300 Hershey's KISSES a minute. The shape of the Hershey's KISSES has not changed, but the name has from the original Sweethearts, to Silvertops, to Silverpoints, and finally Hershey's KISSES. The color of the wrapper changed for the first time at Christmas in 1962 when red and green wrappers joined the familiar silver.

Interesting Facts:

- The streetlights in Hershey, Pennsylvania, are shaped like Hershey's KISSES.

- Hershey has two Hershey's KISSMOBILE Cruisers that travel the United States sharing the message *Every Day Deserves a Kiss.*

More than 5,555 Dum Dum suckers are cranked out each minute.

That is more than 1 billion Dum Dum suckers a year by the Spangler Candy Company. Where did the name *lollipop* originate? A candy maker, George Smith, attached a stick to some hard candy and called it a lollypop, which was the name of his favorite racehorse, Lolly Pop. Why name a candy *Dum Dum*? Apparently, even early candy makers knew that the name of the candy was very important. Dum Dum was believed to be a name that any kid could pronounce and ask for by name. Hard-candy lollipops are made of very simple ingredients: water, sugar, corn syrup, flavoring, and malic or citric acid.

People are spending $954 on chewing gum every minute.

Americans may think that they invented chewing gum, but humans have been chewing an assortment of gums, resins, and latex secretions of plants for thousands of years. The first commercial chewing gum in the United States was State of Maine Spruce Gum in 1850. The best gum base is chicle, which comes from the sap of the sapodilla tree, a tropical rain forest tree. Today, the gum base of chewing gum is made of some chicle and mostly of other natural latex or plastic. The gum base is what is left over after all the sugar and flavor is gone.

Interesting Facts:

- It is illegal to make, import, sell, or chew gum in Singapore.
- Turkey has the most chewing gum manufacturing companies in the world.
- Bubble gum was first introduced in 1928.
- Bubble gum is pink because it was the only color the inventor had left.
- Juicy Fruit and Spearmint gum flavors were first marketed in 1893.

Each minute, 100 rolls of Lifesavers are made.

Why were Lifesavers invented? Clarence Crane wanted a nonmelting candy to sell in the summer when his chocolate sales were slow. In 1912, Clarence invented a round, flat peppermint candy with a hole punched in the center. Clarence sold his Lifesaver business to two New York businessmen who decide to improve the Lifesaver by wrapping it in the now familiar tinfoil. The tinfoil kept the candy from losing its flavor. If you are bored, get a pack of Wint-O-Green Lifesavers and go into a room with a mirror and darken the room. Next, take out a Lifesaver and bite it in half, then keep biting it and try not to get the pieces wet. Did you see any sparks? The flashes are cause by a process called triboluminescence.

Activity 1

Marshmallow Catapult Challenge

How good are you at using a catapult? The catapult was an engineering marvel of the Middle Ages. You can make a homemade catapult using a plastic spoon. You will need one plastic spoon, one large bowl, a piece of string, and a bag of miniature marshmallows for this challenge. First, use the string to make a circle one foot (30 cm) in diameter. Next, walk 5 feet (150 cm) away from the circle. Take several miniature marshmallows from the bag and place one at a time in the plastic spoon. Start a one-minute timer and see how many marshmallows you can land inside the circle in that minute by using the spoon to launch the marshmallows. When you get good at that, then try to catapult the marshmallows into a large bowl at the same distance. You can also try using cereal and dry beans.

Activity 2

Squirrel Food Hunt

Have you ever seen a squirrel taking a nap or sitting perfectly still for long? Probably not, because squirrels are one of the planet's busiest animals. But why are they so busy? Food. It takes a lot of energy to keep their bodies scurrying around and leaping from branch to branch. Therefore, when the weather is nice, they have to gather enough food for the winter months when trees and plants have stopped producing food. Since they don't have refrigerators, they must bury their food in the ground so that it can be eaten later. Then, once winter comes, it's time to run around again, trying to remember where they buried everything.

How good are you at finding things? Do you think you could find your buried food before your energy gets too low and you freeze? Get a friend or a family member and choose who wants to be a fall squirrel and who wants to be a winter squirrel. Fall squirrel takes 10 objects (the smaller the better so they are more like the nuts a squirrel would bury—marbles, coins, paper clips) and has one minute to hide them in a room or around your house while the winter squirrel waits outside. Once the minute is up, the winter squirrel has one minute to find as many of the objects as he or she can. Then, switch roles. Remember, the fall squirrel doesn't want the winter squirrel to die by not finding enough food, so he or she must not get too tricky in hiding the objects; however, the objects must be covered or other animals might get the food before winter squirrel.

POP CULTURE

Every minute, 358 sticks of lipstick are made.

Ever since the ancient Babylonians started the practice around 5,000 years ago, people have been smearing their lips with different colors. Now, it is just as popular as ever. Today, lipstick is made from various oils, waxes, and dyes, but that was not always the case. In ancient Egypt, many people got sick from an ingredient used to make their lipsticks (a reddish-purple dye called fucus); Cleopatra had hers made from crushed beetles and ants. In addition to using plants and chemicals to provide the color of lipstick, fish scales have also been used to make lips shine.

Every minute of the day, 1,714 Lego pieces are manufactured and 9,539 youngsters are playing with the blocks. How long have those 9,539 children been playing with Legos? Ten years? Twenty? How about since 1949? That makes the plastic blocks more than half a century old. Speaking of old, do you think you are too old to play with Legos? Many people have never grown out of playing; there is even a group called "**AFOL**" (Adult Fans of Legos). And they are not just for playing, either. Lego structures are currently hanging in art galleries, have been used in music videos, and have even been used to build padlocks, pendulum clocks, and inkjet printers that actually work!

Every minute, 72 Super Soakers are sold.

The Super Soaker is one of the most popular water guns sold today. The first Super Soaker was called the "Power Drencher" and it was the first water gun to use air pressure. Lonnie Johnson, an aerospace engineer, designed the Super Soaker. Johnson accidentally discovered the mechanism behind the Super Soaker while working on a heat pump system. He designed a prototype, brought it home, and was trying it out in the bathroom when he noticed how strong the water was squirted from it. He thought that this might be a good idea for a water gun. After working six years on the Super Soaker, he put it on the market in 1988.

Each minute, 180 Barbies are sold.

Barbie's full name is Barbie Millicent Roberts, and she is from Willows, Wisconsin, and went to Willows High School. She has 6 siblings, 2 cousins, and more than 101 friends and acquaintances. She has had 38 pets, including a panda, chimpanzee, giraffe, zebra, and lion cub. Barbie has always been a busy woman. During the 47 years since she was created, she has pursued more than 40 different careers. She has been an astronaut, paleontologist, Olympic swimmer, and a presidential candidate. Barbie is also an international phenomenon. Barbies have been created to represent more than 45 different countries and cultures. Barbie was introduced in Europe in 1961, with an Italian doll as the first international Barbie. The first black and Hispanic Barbies were introduced in 1980. Barbie is marketed in 150 nations around the globe. The first Barbie dolls cost $3, and 351,000 were sold the first year.

Fourteen Silly Putty Eggs are made a minute—but none would have been made if not for an accident.

That's right; Silly Putty was created accidentally by scientists trying to create a rubber substitute during World War II. Amazingly, the same accident happened to two different scientists working in two separate labs: James Wright of General Electric and Dr. Earl Warrick of the Dow Corning Corporation. While Silly Putty made its fame as a toy, the Massachusetts Institute of Technology's Web page on inventions claims it can have a variety of more practical uses. Around the house, it can be used to stabilize wobbly furniture and pick up dirt and pet hair. It was even used by the *Apollo 8* space mission to help secure tools in zero gravity.

In China, 50 trees are cut down to produce 85,851 chopsticks each minute.

This means around 45 billion pairs of disposable chopsticks are thrown away every year. That's 25 million trees! Luckily for trees, chopsticks are not only made out of wood. Other materials used to make chopsticks include bamboo, metal, bone, ivory, jade, plastic, silver, and gold. Nobody knows exactly how long people have been using chopsticks to eat, but they are believed to be somewhere between 3,000 and 5,000 years old. Why use chopsticks instead of forks and knives? Some believe that, by avoiding stabbing and cutting at food while eating, a more peaceful atmosphere is created when sharing a meal with friends and family.

Americans are buying $208,334 worth of clothes—why so much?

Clothes—why we wear them and what they mean—have evolved greatly over the thousands of years since humans first put them on. When was the last time you wanted a new shirt only because it would protect you from the sun's rays or keep you warm from a winter's wind? While clothes still cover and protect us, they have also become symbols of status and communicators of our beliefs and opinions. Organic-grown cotton clothes are now available in stores and online businesses.

Organic cotton is grown without the use of pesticides and artificial fertilizers. Natural fertilizers and compost and natural pest control like the use of ladybugs that kill harmful insect pests are used.

SHOP 'TIL YOU DROP

Eager readers purchased 1,111 copies each minute on the first day of sale of *Harry Potter and the Half-Blood Prince*, book six in J. K. Rowling's popular Harry Potter series. That was on July 16, 2006. The Harry Potter craze actually started in 1998 when the first book, *Harry Potter and the Sorcerer's Stone*, was published. The second and third books in the series soon followed in the spring and fall of 1999. In 2000, three million copies of *Harry Potter and the Goblet of Fire* were sold in the first 48 hours of release, making it the fastest-selling book in history. This record was surpassed in 2003 by *Harry Potter and the Order of the Phoenix*. The Harry Potter books have been translated into 61 languages and are sold in more than 200 countries. The total number of books sold has surpassed a quarter of a billion.

On the first day of sale, 5,556 copies of *Finding Nemo* DVDs were sold every minute.

Finding Nemo is the best-selling DVD of all time. *Finding Nemo* was the world's highest-grossing animated film of all time and the ninth highest-grossing film ever. The main character, Nemo, is a clown fish or anemone fish. Nemo was an *Amphiprion ocellaris* clown fish; these live in the tropical Pacific Ocean and grow 3.2 inches (8.1 centimeters) long. Clown fish live in a mutual relationship with sea anemones. The clown fish protects the sea anemone from predators, and the anemone returns the favor by letting the clown fish hide among its tentacles.

On the first day of sale, 3,472 copies of *The Incredibles* DVD were sold every minute.

Pixar Animation Studios produced *The Incredibles*, as well as six other highly successful animated films: *Toy Story*, *A Bug's Life*, *Toy Story 2*, *Monsters, Inc.*, *Finding Nemo*, and *Cars*. *Toy Story* was the very first completely computer-generated animated movie. Computer animation is also called Computer Generated Imagery, or CGI. One of the most difficult things to do in CGI is to make a human. Humans have very complex body structures, facial expressions, and motions. The challenge in the animated film industry is to make a movie that has realistic human motion, human body features, and human interactions. Filmmakers use very fast and powerful computers and specialized software to create animated films. To make an animated movie, television show, or video game sequence look real, it takes a lot of detailed work.

THAT'S INCREDIBLE

179

One hundred iPods are sold every minute, but the iPod is only the central figure of the larger iPod ecosystem.

There are currently more than 2,000 accessories available to improve the appearance and performance of the iPod. The iPod accessory market has grown into a billion-dollar business. iPods were meant to be mobile and now they can be found just about everywhere and embedded in everything. At first, the accessories were simple: colored slips, better headphones, and docking stations. Now, the iPod has moved well beyond the simple, single-colored slips to expensive, designer patterns by Coach. It is likely tomorrow's children will have their first iPod experience before they take their first steps with the iPod stroller.

About 1,900 iTunes songs are downloaded each minute around the world.

More than 2 billion iTunes songs have been downloaded since they were first introduced in April 2003. The number of people visiting the iTunes site increased from 6.1 million in 2004 to 20.7 million in 2005. Close to 14 percent of active Internet users are frequently using the service. Teenagers visit the site most often and are twice as apt to use it than any other age group. In October 2005, iTunes offered video downloads of music videos and five TV shows that were available 24 hours after they were aired. Some of the past season's shows were also offered. In 2007, the iTunes Music Store offered more than 350 television shows for download, which included shows from Discovery Channel, Comedy Central, MTV, and Fox.

Each minute, 152 people join MySpace.com—that means more than 60 million people have posted their profiles since 2003. It continues to thrive as one of the Internet's most popular destinations. MySpace has become much more than just a cultural fad. Unlike past fads like the hula hoop and pet rock, MySpace is not just a part of popular culture, it is helping to create and determine pop culture through the posting of movies and music. There are 50,000 groups, including fashion, health, sports and recreation, music, film, and fitness. The members are split almost evenly between male (50.2 percent) and female (49.8 percent), with the main demographic being ages 16 to 34.

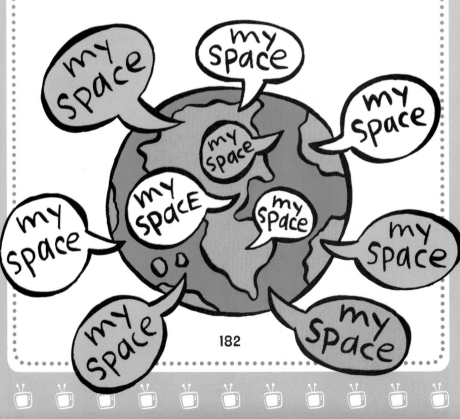

182

Babbling SpongeBob Dolls sold at a rate of seven per minute—he can say more than 20 phrases, but can he say all of his names?

SpongeBob's international popularity has grown so much that he is now televised in more than 17 countries, and his name has been translated into several languages including: SpongeBob SpongeHead (German), SpongeBob the Square (Hebrew), Bob the Sponge (French), SpongeBob Square (Danish, Swedish, and Norwegian), SquareSquare SquareBob (Korean), SpongeBob WidePants (Lithuanian), Bob Sponge (Spanish), and Bob the Little Sponge SquarePants (Greek). SpongeBob was going to be named Spongeboy, but the name had already been trademarked.

SpongeBob was created by Steve Hillenburg, a marine biologist and science teacher who decided to take a class in cartooning.

Dora the Explorer's latest 3 DVDs were purchased at the rate of about 12 a minute in 2004.

What does the Spanish word *exploradora* mean? It means "female explorer" and that is where Dora got her name. Since Dora broke onto the scene in 2000, she has captured the interest of millions of children around the world. Dora is brave, loyal, kind, and adventurous—all the characteristics of a great role model. By the end of 2005, Dora sold more than $4 billion of merchandise in just the United States. Dora's products range from DVDs and dolls to Band-Aids and a talking backpack. Dora the Explorer became the first Latina balloon character in the 79th Macy's Thanksgiving Day Parade on November 21, 2005.

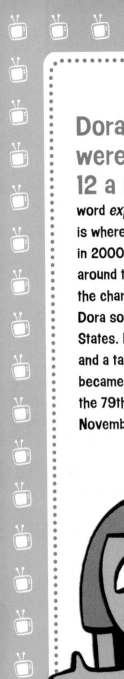

Bratz dolls are sold worldwide at the rate of 238 a minute and are famous for showing off the latest fashions and trends popular today. But did you know many believe the doll to be humankind's oldest toy? Dolls were not only for playing, either. Since the 15th century, dolls began being used as gifts of goodwill between the leaders of countries and, even more important, as instruments to promote and spread fashion. In colonial times, there were no television ads to promote the latest fashions so designers would decorate dolls with their latest lines of clothing and then send them off to the colonies so people could keep up-to-date with the latest European styles.

The Claymation™ movie *Wallace and Gromit* has 1,440 frames of animation a minute—in other words, for every second you watch in the movie, 24 frames of film flash by.

It may not seem like it, but a lot of time-consuming work goes into each *Wallace and Gromit* production. In order to create the appearance of fluid movement, the clay stars must be moved very slightly for each frame filmed. How much work is it? During a typical day of filming, only 30 frames of film are shot. That is 1.25 seconds of film a day! It took five years to make the movie *Wallace and Gromit and the Curse of the Were-Rabbit.* The film had 30 miniature sets. The filmmakers used 2.8 tons (2 metric tons) of Plasticine in 42 colors. The production crew used 44 pounds (20 kilograms) of glue every month to stick down the characters to the sets.

The world's fastest typist typed 150 words a minute for a period of 50 minutes—that's 2.5 words every second!

Consider how amazing that rate is: A beginning typist usually types at a rate of 20 words per minute, and 60 words per minute is considered advanced. That puts the record at 2.5 times faster. Still aren't impressed? Instead of typing at a keyboard, think about riding in a car. If you were traveling in a "fast" car that travels at 60 miles (96.5 kilometers) per hour, then the world's fastest would blow past you traveling 150 miles (241.4 kilometers) per hour! Even more impressive, the world's fastest typist, Barbara Blackburn, can type at rates of 170 words a minute for periods shorter than 50 minutes and has reached a maximum speed of 212 words a minute.

☼ POP CULTURE ☼

People are spending $26,000 every minute on ring tones—wow, we must be addicted to ring tones!

But humans are not the only ones who like to imitate catchy tunes. Recently, it has been discovered that birds are starting to imitate the ring tones. A large variety of city-dwelling birds are picking up the sounds of ring tones from the increasing number of cell phone-carrying citizens. As the birds attempt to familiarize themselves with their environment, they listen for sounds in hopes of finding future mates. Once they hear the ring tones, male birds mistake them for female birds and try to mimic their sounds in hopes of meeting them. Next time you hear the "Crazy Frog," it might not be a phone—it could be a bird looking for a date! Maybe it would be easier if the bird just picked up a phone and called.

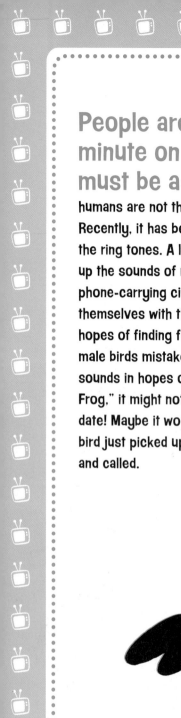

TWEET

More than 69,444 people are watching YouTube video clips every minute—that is more than the entire population of Santa Fe, New Mexico!

Not only does YouTube's current popularity dwarf most other Web sites, its meteoric rise in popularity leaves others in its dust. Currently, approximately 35,000 new videos are being uploaded every day (about 24 every minute), so who knows if it will ever stop growing. The daily total is 100 million people watching. Men are 20 percent more apt to visit YouTube than women. Visitors between the ages of 12 and 17 are the most frequent users and are 1.5 times more likely to use YouTube than any other age group.

189

Activity 1

Commercial Overload

Do you stick around to watch the commercials during your favorite television shows? Probably not, but advertisers know this so they try to make their commercials as quick and catchy as possible. Television networks also know the value of time; that is why they sell advertising time by the second. Next time you are watching television, wait for a commercial break. Once the break begins, set your minute timer and see how many ads flash by in the space of a minute. Were you surprised at the number? You can also turn this activity into an experiment. Draw a table with different types of television programs (sitcoms, dramas, cartoons, news, sports, etc.) and times (morning, afternoon, and evening). Count the number of commercials that occur according to program and time. Which programs and times have the most commercials per minute? Why do you think this is the case? For additional research, you can get online and search for more information about television commercials. What are the rates networks charge for commercials? What is the most an advertiser ever paid for a commercial?

Activity 2

Lickety-split Challenge

How many times have you taken a cream-filled cookie like an Oreo, broken it in half, and licked out the cream filling? This challenge is to open a cream-filled cookie and see if you can lick the filling out in one minute. You may not use your teeth in the challenge, only your tongue. If you can lick out the filling in less than a minute, then see how many cream fillings you can lick out in one minute. Next, try this challenge with other cream-filled cookies to see if one kind of cream filling is easier to lick clean. Use a Double-Stuffed Oreo and compare with two regular Oreos, to see if the Double-Stuffed has twice the filling.

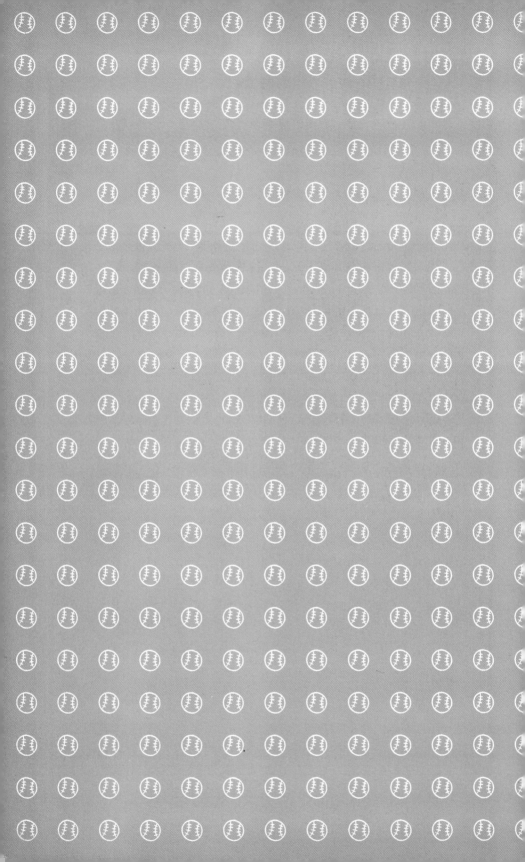

Lance Armstrong can produce 400 watts of power per minute and breathe in 148 quarts (140 liters) of air. His heart beats 200 times a minute and can pump 9 gallons (34 liters) of blood each minute. An average man can only pump 5 gallons (19 liters) per minute. Lance Armstrong is one phenomenal human specimen from a purely physical viewpoint. His heart is larger than most humans, and his lung capacity is extremely large. These two physical characteristics give him an incredible edge in sustained cardiovascular exercise such as cycling and running. Lance Armstrong started with a strong genetic makeup, but training is the other part of his strength and endurance. Lance's body also produces less lactic acid when exercising and can get rid of it more efficiently. Lactic acid in the muscles is what makes them sore.

In one minute, a **NASCAR** pit crew can change 16 tires that weight 75 pounds (34.1 kilograms) each.

It takes a lot of people to keep a car in top shape, but **NASCAR** rules state that only seven people can go "over the wall" to work on a car during a pit stop. The seven members of an active pit crew are the front tire changer, rear tire changer, jack man (he jacks up the car so the tires can be changed), gas man, gas catch man (he uses a "catch can" to catch any gas that overflows from the gas tank once it is full), and two tire carriers (one carries tires to the front and one to the back; they both help to guide the tires in place for the tire changers).

A skydiver travels 2 miles (3.2 kilometers) per minute and an experienced skydiver in a dive or "stand up" travels up to 3 miles (4.8 kilometers) per minute—that's 120 to 180 miles (193.1 to 289.6 kilometers) per hour!

But that is nothing compared to what Joseph Kittinger did on August 16, 1960. On that day, Kittinger jumped from a balloon he piloted 102,800 feet (31,333.5 meters) and in doing so, he set four world records: highest parachute jump, longest freefall, fastest speed traveled by a human through the atmosphere, and highest balloon flight. During his jump, he reached a top speed of 618 miles (994.4 kilometers) per hour! Joseph fell 84,800 feet (25,847.1 meters) before he opened his parachute—that is more than twice as high as commercial airliners fly!

Every minute, roughly 115 soccer balls are made and 61 of them are in Pakistan.

Of the balls made in Pakistan, 75 percent are made in Sialkot, a city of approximately 3 million in the north of the country. Sialkot's sporting goods industry dates back to the late 19th century. According to legend, it all began when an Englishman accidentally broke his tennis racquet. Since it would take too long to have a replacement sent all the way from England, he took it to a local craftsman. The local craftsman did such a great job in repairing his racquet an entire industry was born. The town first specialized in tennis racquets, but it did not take long before it became a center for manufacturing cricket bats, sporting uniforms, and, of course, soccer balls.

Baseballs are manufactured at the rate of 1.3 per minute.

Until 1974 baseballs were made out of horsehides. Now, cowhides are used due to a decrease in supply of horsehide. The manufacturing of baseballs is now highly regulated (a cork core, two rubber layers, 121 yards [110.6 meters] of four-ply yarn, 45 yards [41.1 meters] of three-ply yarn, an additional 53 yards [48.5 meters] of three-ply yarn, 150 yards [137.2 meters] of a polyester-cotton blend yarn, two pieces of figure-eight-shaped cowhide, and 88 inches [2.2 meters] of red cotton thread put through 216 raised stitches to hold it all together). Each major league baseball team in America buys 18,000 baseballs a year. Since there are 30 major league teams, the total number of baseballs bought is 540,000.

The Wilson Sport Company makes 95 tennis balls each minute.

Tennis balls are made up of two parts, the core and the outer cloth. The core consists of two rubber halves held together by glue. A cloth of either white or green is then stretched over the core and attached with an adhesive. There are two types of balls approved by the International Tennis Federation (ITF): pressurized and nonpressurized. A pressurized tennis ball has its core filled with air or nitrogen, but don't buy one unless you plan on using it. The air slowly escapes and the ball loses much of its bounce over time. Nonpressurized balls have a thicker rubber core so the air inside does not escape nearly as quickly and it will bounce like new for much longer.

Golf balls are produced at a rate of 4,770 per minute.

While, today, golf balls are made using space-age plastics and rubbers, the first golf balls used more than 500 years ago were made of solid wood. In the early 17th century, a new ball was introduced, the featherie. It was made of boiled feathers wrapped in a leather cover. Because it took so long to make, they were very expensive, but golfers used them for nearly 200 years! Everything changed once rubber was discovered by European traders and made available from the tropics. It was soon found that golf balls made of hardened rubber would travel farther when hit and could be made much quicker and cheaper than the featherie.

A Thoroughbred horse goes 120 paces a minute during a horse race.

Those four slender legs are carrying more than 1,000 pounds (454.5 kilograms) of horse during those quick paces. And they can reach top speeds of 35 to 40 miles (56 to 64 kilometers) per hour! Horses are unique because they are not measured using feet or meters, they are measured with hands. One hand is measured as the distance between the index and pinky fingers (approximately 4 inches or 10.12 centimeters). A typical Thoroughbred stands 16 hands (64 inches or 1.6 meters) high from the ground to the top of the withers (the highest point of the horse's back). How many hands tall are you?

During a qualifying lap, NASCAR racers have traveled more than 3 miles (4.8 kilometers) in one minute. Before restrictor plates, Bill Elliot was clocked at 212.8 miles (342.4 kilometers) per hour in 1987. He also holds the record with restrictor plates with a speed of 199.4 miles (320.8 kilometers) per hour. Restrictor plates are now required in cars during races at Daytona International Speedway and Talladega Superspeedway to help control the speed of the cars. NASCAR uses restrictor plates to reduce speed and make the races safer for the drivers and fans, but many believe the use of the plates makes the races even more dangerous because the reduction in speed and acceleration makes it more difficult to pass other cars.

In the 2005 Tour de France, Lance Armstrong's average speed was 2,277 feet (694 meters) per minute, which is the fastest time in history.

The 2006 disqualified winner, Floyd Landis, had an average speed of 2,220 feet (676.7 meters) per minute, the third fastest on record. The total time for the 2006 Tour was 89 hours, 39 minutes, and 30 seconds. The average rider was 5 feet 10 inches (1.8 meters) tall and weighed 157 pounds (71.4 kilograms). The heaviest rider weighed 209 pounds (95 kilograms) and the lightest was 126 pounds (57.3 kilograms). The tallest rider was 6 feet 5 inches (2 meters) and the shortest was 5 feet 2 inches (1.6 meters).

NFL footballs are made by Wilson at the rate of 3.5 every minute.

They are made out of leather, not pigskin. The term pigskin goes back to when football was first played in the late 19th century. Before vulcanized rubber (a chemical process that makes rubber springier, harder, and more durable) was commonly available, pigs' bladders were readily available and easily transformed into a ball by blowing air into them. Since asking friends to throw around a "pigskin" rather than a "pig bladder" sounds more inviting, the name stuck. The name has lasted even though today strips of cow leather are used to cover the rubber bladders of footballs.

Darren Powell of Australia travels 2.2 miles (3.5 kilometers) a minute downhill on a snowboard—which means he holds the world record for highest speed on a snowboard. Did you know the first snowboard was called a "Snurfer"? It was invented in 1965 when Sherman Poppen saw one of his daughters standing up on her sled as she rode it down a hill. Originally, the Snurfer was two skis bound together with a string tied to the nose of the boards so the rider could control them. People loved the new Snurfers so much that they began having competitions. Eventually, in 1979, Jack Burton Carpenter showed up at a competition with a Snurfer that he had modified so that it did not have a string to control it. Instead, it had bindings for the rider's feet so it could be controlled much like a skateboard; and the modern snowboard was born.

A tennis serve by Venus Williams travels 2.1 miles (3.4 kilometers) in a minute and Andy Roddick's goes 2.6 miles (4.2 kilometers) during a minute. That's 127.4 miles (205 kilometers) per hour for Williams and 153 miles (246.2 kilometers) per hour for Roddick. Before metal racquets began to replace wooden ones in the late 1960s, the world's fastest serve belonged to Pancho Gonzalez. His serve reached speeds of 112 miles (180.2 kilometers) per hour. His serve made him so dominant that he was the world's number one tennis player for nine years in the 1950s and 1960s. With today's modern, lightweight racquets, serves routinely exceed Gonzalez's 112 miles (180.2 kilometers) per hour, but none have matched his dominance.

Tomas Leandersson of Sweden made six bowling strikes in one minute.

That is an amazing feat considering that making 12 consecutive strikes is a perfect game in bowling. Plus it takes time and concentration to be able to knock over all ten pins with one roll of the bowling ball. Dutch settlers probably brought bowling to America; however, they used nine pins. After colonial laws were made against ninepin, the tenpin game was created. Bowling is one of the most popular sports in the world today. Bowling is enjoyed by 95 million people in 90 countries worldwide.

Interesting Facts:

- Japan has the largest bowling center with 141 lanes.
- Bowling was an Olympic sport in the 1936 games in Berlin, Germany.
- The Bowling Hall of Fame is in St. Louis, Missouri.

The fastest average speed of a winning car at the Indianapolis 500, driven by Dutchman Arie Luyendyk in 1990, was going 3.1 miles (5 kilometers) a minute.

That's 1.24 laps a minute with an average speed of 186 miles (299.3 kilometers) per hour. How long is a lap? The oval at the Indianapolis Speedway is 2.5 miles (4 kilometers) long. Not impressed? Did you know that there is enough room inside the oval to put the All England Lawn Tennis and Croquet Club (where the Wimbledon Championships are held), the Roman Colosseum, Yankee Stadium, the Rose Bowl Stadium, Churchill Downs, and the entire Vatican City?

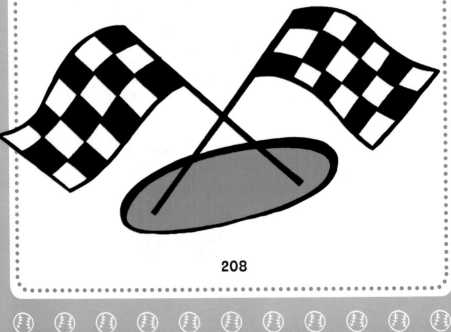

Buddy Lee, a former U.S. Olympic wrestler, can jump rope at the rate of 360 jumps a minute. That is incredible since 115 to 140 jumps a minute is considered to be sufficient for a good workout. Frank P. Oliveri holds the endurance record for jumping rope. He skipped for 31 hours, 46 minutes in May 1989 with a few restroom breaks. The record for the most people jumping a rope at the same time is 260 people. They were students at the Yorkton Regional High School in Canada and in 1992 had to jump 12 turns of the rope.

Major League Baseball player Alex Rodriguez earns $864.20 a minute during the season, with a game lasting an average of three hours.

Is he worth it? Perhaps fans will never be in complete agreement, but his numbers are as unique as his salary. Before you make a decision, consider these facts: He was the youngest player to reach 400 home runs (29 years and 316 days old) and 450 home runs (30 years and 359 days old); he has the most home runs hit by a right-handed hitter in Yankee Stadium, passing Joe DiMaggio and Gary Sheffield; and he is the only player to hold single-season home run records at two separate positions (shortstop and third base). Maybe most amazingly, he is on pace to become the all-time leader in home runs, RBIs, runs, and hits.

A 150-pound (68.2-kilogram) marathon runner will burn 20.6 calories a minute during the 26.2-mile race. The world record time for a marathon is 2 hours, 4 minutes, and 55 seconds. That is a pace of approximately 1,107 feet (337.4 meters) every minute! The Boston Marathon is the oldest annual marathon in the world at 110 years (2006). More than 20,000 runners are expected in the 2007 run. The New York City Marathon is the largest with more than 85,000 applicants and more than 36,000 crossing the finish line in 2005.

In the World Memory Championship, the contestants have 1 minute to recall the order of a deck of cards.

It is believed that soon, some of the planet's top memorizers will be able to memorize an entire pack of 52 playing cards in 30 seconds. Every year, memory competitions are held all over the world. There usually is not a lot of money to be made, but the rank of grand master of memory is highly sought after. As of 2005, there were only 36 grand masters of memory in the entire world. In order to attain the title, one must be able to memorize 1,000 digits in under an hour; the exact order of ten shuffled decks of playing cards in an hour; and the exact order of one deck of cards in less than two minutes.

Do not leave a Sumo wrestling match for one minute. Why?

Rarely do Sumo wrestling matches last for more than one minute— most only last a few seconds. The Sumatori or Sumo wrestler is greatly respected in Japan. Sumo wrestling is the national sport in Japan. The Sumo wrestler will lose the match if he touches the ground with any part of his body other than his feet, touches the outside of the circle, uses an illegal hold or his *mawashi* (belt) becomes completely undone. They have to grow their hair long to form a topknot. When in public, they are expected to wear traditional Japanese clothes. The Sumo wrestlers eat huge amounts of food and go to bed right after eating so they can gain more weight.

Activity 1

Crunch Time

The last minute of a basketball game can be one of the most exciting minutes in all of sports. Due to its importance and high level of stress, it is often labeled crunch time. For many players, it is how they perform during this crucial minute that determines how their fans and history will remember them. How many baskets do you think you can make in a minute? Write down a number, set your timer for a minute, and start shooting. Did you get your number? Lower? Keep practicing and see if you can make it. Higher? Raise your number and see if you can make that. Now try making basket at different distances, 2 yards (2 meters) and 4 yards (about 4 meters) and so on. Once you have practiced enough, grab a friend and play a minute game. You have one minute to make a basket and your friend has one minute to defend you. Be careful, though, because however much time is still on the clock after you make your basket, your friend will have that much time to take a shot of his or her own.

Activity 2

On Your Mark, Get Set. . .

The push-up is a classic exercise that has been used for years to build upper body strength. It requires a number of muscles in your chest and arms to move your body up and down. But what about just holding your body up? If you are not moving, are your muscles still working? The "push-up position" does not sound like it would be very difficult to perform, but you might be surprised. Get down on the floor in the push-up position, with your arms straight, but don't drop. See if you can hold yourself in this "up" position for one minute. How do your arms feel afterward? If you were able to hold the position for a full minute, how much longer do you think you could hold it for? After you try the "up" position for a minute, you can also try the "down" position. For this one, start out the same way, except lower yourself partway down so your arms are bent but your body is not touching the floor. See if you can hold this position for a minute. Now how are your arms doing? Next, see how many push-ups you can do in a minute. Practice your push-ups daily and at the end of a month see if you can do more than when you first started.

Source Notes

Allergy Capital
American Beverage Association
BBC
Blue Moo
Bowling Museum
Brach's
British Broadcasting Center
Campbell's Soup
CNET
Connecticut Department of Environmental Protection
Cornell Chronicles
Cray Computers
Discover Magazine
Dorafansite.com
Dunkin' Donuts
Earth Policy Institute
Gemini Observatory
Georgia Aquarium
Gourmetcoffeeclub.com
Honey.com
Hypertextbook
Idaho Fish and Game Department
Indy 500
Insect Zoo, Mississippi State University
iSoaker.com
Jack in the Box
Jellybelly.com
Jet Propulsion Lab
KidsHealth
Krispy Kreme
Library of Congress
Massachusetts Lobstermen's Association
Mattel
Maui-info.com

⏰ EVERY MINUTE ON EARTH ⏰

NASA

National Association of Pizza Operators

National Hot Dog and Sausage Council

National Peanut Board

National Zoo

Necco.com

New Brunswick.net

Nikon Microscopy

P&G Hair Care Research Center

PC World

Peanutbutter.com

Pet Food Institute

Pez.com

Recording Industry Association of America

San Diego Zoo

Scholastic Inc.

Spaceflightnow

Spangler Candy

SR-71 Online

U.S. Air Force

U.S. Environmental Protection Agency

U.S. Fish and Wildlife Service

U.S. Geologic Survey

U.S. Mint

U.S. Patent and Trademark Office

U.S. Popcorn Board

U.S. Treasury

University of Illinois Extension

University of Kentucky

Wildbird Magazine

World Book Encyclopedia

World Book Encyclopedia New Scientists

Worm Watch

Wrigley

Index

☀ EVERY MINUTE ON EARTH ☀

Index

Index

☀ EVERY MINUTE ON EARTH ☀

Index